Household Hints
for
Upstairs, Downstairs, and
All Around the House

Household Hints for Upstairs, Downstairs, and All Around the House

Carol Rees

An Owl Book

HENRY HOLT AND COMPANY

NEW YORK

The suggestions made in this book are intended for the reader's use as possible solutions to frequently encountered household problems. Neither the author, the publisher, nor the distributor of this publication can assume responsibility for the efficacy of the procedures described in all cases, nor are the procedures intended to suggest that success will be encountered at all times. As with all matters, the author, publisher, and distributor of this publication recommend thoughtful common sense in the application of all suggestions made in the book.

Artwork by Susan Coleman

Published by Henry Holt and Company, Inc.,
115 West 18th Street, New York, New York 10011.
Published in Canada by Fitzhenry & Whiteside Limited,
195 Allstate Parkway, Markham, Ontario L3R 4T8.

Library of Congress Cataloging-in-Publication Data
Rees, Carol.
Household hints for upstairs, downstairs, and all around the house.
Reprint. Originally published: Hints for upstairs, downstairs, and all around the house. Waycross, Ga.:
C. Rees, c1982.
"An Owl Book."
Includes index.
1. Home economics.   2. House cleaning.   I. Title.
TX158.R44   1988   640   87-28864
ISBN 0-8050-0765-2 (pbk.)

Henry Holt books are available at special discounts for bulk purchases for sales promotions, premiums, fund-raising, or educational use. Special editions or book excerpts can also be created to specification. For details contact:
Special Sales Director, Henry Holt and Company, Inc.,
115 West 18th Street, New York, New York 10011.

First published by Carol Rees Publications in 1982.
First Owl Book Edition—1988

Printed in the United States of America
3   5   7   9   10   8   6   4   2

This book is dedicated to Ruth Crichton, Dot Gibson, and Joanna Seaman. Without their tireless efforts and constant support and encouragement, this book would not have been possible.

AUTHOR'S NOTE

This book was born of desperation. As a bride I shrank my husband's sweaters down to doll-size while burning the supper. As a mother I despaired over children's squabbles while washing the dog. As a working wife I realized that I needed to put my collection of household hints, which had been stuck around in every nook and cranny for twenty-eight years, into a handy reference. *Household Hints for Upstairs, Downstairs, and All Around the House* is the result.

Having these hints in one spot has been a help to me, I have used them and continue to use them as I juggle family, home, and career and deal with the mishaps of all three.

I know that these household hints will help you too.

I wish to thank the following individuals and businesses for their contributions to this book:

Bailey Monument Company · Jean Baldwin · Crawford Jewelers · Georgia Cooperative Extension Service: Kate Burke, Vivian Harrington · James E. Hart Jewelers, Inc. · Lyda Long · Bunny Matthews · Barbara Moore · Town and Country Cleaners · Lou Turk

CONTENTS

Household Hints
for
Upstairs, Downstairs, and
All Around the House

Bathrooms

BATHROOMS

CLEANING TOILETS
Scrub stubborn toilet stains with:
1. Sand sprinkled on a wet sponge.
2. A sandstone (which can be bought from a plumbing supply house).
3. An old sand brick.
4. A commercial cleanser containing oxalic acid.

MINERAL STAINS ON SINKS AND TUBS
Pour hydrogen peroxide on the stain, then sprinkle with cream of tartar. Leave this for 30 minutes before scrubbing. Bad stains may require 2 or 3 applications.

CLEANING BATHROOM FIXTURES
Clean bathroom fixtures by scrubbing with one of the following:
1. White vinegar
2. A commercial cleanser containing oxalic acid.
3. Turpentine
4. A commercial cleaner containing trisodium phosphate.
5. Automatic dishwasher detergent.

QUICK BATHROOM CLEAN-UP
1. Keep an old detergent bottle or a spray bottle filled with a water-bleach solution or a water-ammonia solution for quick clean-ups of tubs or showers immediately after bathing.
2. Clean tub easier by covering bottom of the tub with water and adding 1 cup of chlorine bleach. Allow to stand 1 hour.

REMOVING RUST FROM CHROME
Scrub rust spots with grade no. 000 steel wool dipped in kerosene.

BATHROOMS

CLEANING CERAMIC TILE

1. Scrub ceramic tile with a solution of ½ cup ammonia to 1 gallon of hot water.
2. Scrub and polish tile with grade no. 0 or grade no. 1 steel wool.

BATHROOM ODORS

Eliminate bathroom odors by:
1. Lighting a match or candle.
2. Keeping an open box of soda placed in the corner.
3. Keeping a small dish of vinegar on the vanity.

MOISTURE IN BATHROOMS

Keep 2 or 3 pieces of charcoal in the bathroom linen closet to absorb excess moisture.

SOAP SLIVERS

1. Put soap slivers in a plastic cup with a little water for a few days. The soap will become soft and can be used as a liquid soap.
2. Place soap slivers in a small net bag. When the bag is filled, keep it in your soap dish. When needed, wet with water and use as you would a bar of soap.

REMOVING TUB APPLIQUÉS AND ADHESIVES

1. Remove appliqué by scrubbing with a cloth dampened in kerosene.
2. After peeling the decal off the tub, scrub the remaining adhesive with a washcloth and cooking oil until all traces of the adhesive are gone.

FOGGED MIRRORS

Use a hair blow dryer to dry the steam off your bathroom mirror.

Carpets and Floors

CARPETS AND FLOORS

ASPHALT TILE
BRICK
CARPETS
CERAMIC TILE
LINOLEUM
VINYL
WOOD

════CARPETS AND FLOORS

CLEANING DIRTY CARPETS
Wet method:
Make suds with a mild detergent and water. Using the suds only, apply with a sponge to a small section of the carpet.

Dry method:
Sprinkle carpet all over with baking soda or cornmeal. After brushing it in, leave on for 30 minutes before vacuuming thoroughly.

KEEPING CARPET CLEAN
Keep carpets clean by vacuuming little-used areas weekly and frequently-used areas daily. For a good cleaning, go over each area 5 or 6 times per cleaning.

SHOE POLISH ON CARPET
Remove shoe polish from carpet by rubbing with a cloth dampened in turpentine or alcohol.

GREASE SPOTS ON CARPET
1. Sprinkle baking soda, corn meal, or baby powder on grease spots immediately. Leave on overnight and then vacuum.
2. Dampen a cloth with lighter fluid and scrub grease spot with a circular motion. Repeat this until grease is removed.

LIPSTICK ON CARPET
Rub the spot with glycerine first, then with undiluted lighter fluid.

MATTED CARPET
The nap on carpet which has become matted by heavy furniture can be restored by steaming. Steam with a steam iron held just over the depressed area for a few seconds, then brush the nap with a stiff brush. Repeat this procedure 2 or 3 times if necessary.

CARPETS AND FLOORS

MUSTARD ON CARPET

After removing as much of the mustard as possible with a knife blade, scrub with one of the following:
1. Cold water
2. 1 teaspoon of a mild detergent to 1 cup water
3. ¼ cup of white vinegar to 1 cup water

CARPET ODORS

Remove carpet odors and give your rooms a refreshing scent by:
1. Sprinkling baking soda over the carpet the night before you plan to vacuum.
2. Putting a few drops of your favorite perfume, oil of peppermint, or any other pleasant-smelling liquid on a tissue. Vacuum this tissue into the cleaner before vacuuming the carpet. This really is a quick way to make your room smell wonderful.

CANDLE WAX ON WOOD FLOORS

Remove candle wax on wood floors by first hardening the wax with an ice cube, and then removing as much of the wax as possible with a table knife. Rub the spot with liquid wax and polish the surface.

PROTECTING WOOD FLOORS

Apply a thin coat of paste wax to a clean, dry floor. Polish with an electric polisher or by rubbing with a brick wrapped in a wool cloth. Rub with the grain of the wood.

CLEANING NEW BRICK FLOORS

Clean a new brick floor with muriatic acid. Scrub muriatic acid on with a stiff brush and rinse with water. After the brick is completely dry, apply a thin coat of sealer for a beautiful finish.

CAUTION: When using muriatic acid, wear rubber gloves and avoid getting on your skin or clothes. If you are working indoors, make sure the room is ventilated.

CARPETS AND FLOORS

CLEANING WOOD FLOORS

Clean wood floors by mopping with a solution of mild detergent and water. Make sure the mop is not too wet to avoid oversoaking the floor. Rinse with clear water. Again, make certain mop is only damp, not wet. Dry the floor with a terry cloth towel. When the floor is completely dry, rewax and polish.

PAINT SPLATTERS ON WOOD, ASPHALT TILE, OR LINOLEUM FLOORS

To remove fresh water-based paint, rub with a cloth dampened in water. To remove fresh oil-based paint, rub gently with fine steel wool dipped in paste wax. To remove dried paint, saturate the spot with boiled linseed oil and let stand for awhile. Wipe the area and remove any remaining paint with a paste made of pumice powder and mineral oil.

GREASE AND TAR ON WOOD OR ASPHALT TILE FLOORS

Remove heavy grease marks and tar from wood or asphalt tile floors by first scraping off the excess and then wiping the residue with a cloth dampened with lighter fluid or charcoal lighter.

CLEANING LINOLEUM AND CERAMIC TILE FLOORS

Scrub flooring with a solution of ½ cup of ammonia and a gallon of hot water. Rinse with clear water.

REMOVING BURNS ON WOOD FLOORS

With a small knife, gently scrape away all the discoloration in the damaged area. When the discoloration has been removed, apply clear fingernail polish and let it harden. Repeat this until the cavity is filled completely level.

15

CARPETS AND FLOORS

MARKS AND OLD WAX ON LINOLEUM, VINYL, AND ASPHALT TILE
Remove scuff marks or ground-in dirt by rubbing lightly with grade no. 2 steel wool.

ASPHALT TILE AND LINOLEUM FLOORING
WARNING: Do not spray oil-base insecticides on asphalt tile or linoleum floors. This type insecticide could damage these floors.

FOOD STAINS ON LINOLEUM, VINYL, AND ASPHALT TILE
Remove food stains by using a commercial cleaner containing trisodium phosphate on the spots. Apply with a sponge and wipe with clear water.

CLEANING SEALED BRICK FLOORS
Wash sealed brick floors with a solution of ½ cup of ammonia to a gallon of hot water.

PET STAINS AND ODORS
Pet stains and odors can be removed from carpets by following this procedure:
1. Blot stain quickly with paper towels.
2. Scrub spot vigorously with a terry cloth towel dipped in white vinegar. Be sure to squeeze excess vinegar out of towel before rubbing.
3. Rub with a circular motion.
4. When dry, fluff nap with a soft brush.

Ceiling to Floor

CEILING TO FLOOR

CEILINGS
CHANDELIERS
DUSTING
FIREPLACES
PAINTING
PICTURE FRAMES
PICTURES
WALLPAPER
WALLS
WINDOWS
WINDOW SHADES
WOOD PANELING
WOODWORK

CEILING TO FLOOR

DUSTING CEILINGS AND PICTURE FRAMES

A very useful tool for dusting ceilings, vents, and picture frames can be made of nylon net and a broom handle. Gather a 6 inch by 24 inch piece of net into a pom-pon and tack this onto the end of a broom handle. You can use this more than you can imagine.

CRYSTAL CHANDELIERS

Make washing a crystal chandelier easier by taking it step-by-step:
1. Remove light bulbs, wash, rinse, and put them aside.
2. Place a folded towel on the bottom of a sink or dishpan. Half fill it with warm water, make suds with castile soap, not detergent.
3. Pad another sink or dishpan, fill with warm water and a few drops of ammonia.
4. Remove crystal prisms and saucers and begin working on a few at a time. Wash with a sponge, rinse, and dry with tissue paper.
5. While bulbs and prisms are removed, wipe the arms of the chandelier with a cloth dampened with the soap suds. Rinse with a fresh, lintless cloth dampened with the ammonia solution. Polish with tissue paper.
6. Replace prisms and dry bulbs.

HANGING PICTURES

Put cellophane tape on the wall before driving a nail. If you should change pictures and need to remove the nail, the tape will keep the paint from peeling off.

REPAIRING ANTIQUE GOLD PICTURE FRAMES

Small nicks in antique gold picture frames can be filled with plastic wood and then rubbed with gold leaf. If the frame has missing pieces of beadwork or missing parts of a three-dimensional design, mold the plastic wood into the desired shape and stick it in place on the frame. When the new pieces are dry, rub with gold leaf to match the rest of the frame.

19

CEILING TO FLOOR ══════

PREVENTING MARS AND SCRATCHES ON WALLS AND WALLPAPER

Prevent your walls and wallpaper from becoming marred and scratched by broom handles and chairs by these methods:

1. Put an athletic sock over the broom handle and secure with a rubber band, then no matter where you prop your broom the walls won't become marred.
2. Glue a narrow strip from a kitchen sponge to the outside back of your chairs. Then when the chairs are pushed against the wall, the sponge will prevent any marring. This is especially helpful for chairs in a child's room or breakfast room.

CLEANING WINDOWS

Clean windows and make them sparkle by using any one of the following:

1. Rubbing alcohol
2. White vinegar
3. Glycerine applied with a moist cloth
4. Mixture of ½ cup of ammonia, ½ cup of vinegar, and 2 tablespoons of cornstarch

Paper towels or newspapers make excellent lint-free "cloths" for washing windows.

REMOVING PAINT FROM WINDOW PANES

Remove paint splatters on window panes with hot vinegar.

STICKING DRAWERS AND WINDOWS

Rub sticking drawers and windows with candles, paraffin, or soap for easier opening.

CLEANING FIREPLACES

Dirty brick or stone fireplaces can be cleaned with:

1. 1 cup dishwasher detergent and 1 quart of water
2. Chlorine bleach
3. Soap pads

Rinse well and allow to air dry.

CLEANING WINDOW SHADES

Place pulled-out shade flat on a kitchen table or counter which has been covered with a plastic cloth. Wash with a sponge dipped in warm water and detergent moving from the top to the bottom. Textured shades may need to be scrubbed gently with a soft brush. Rinse well with clean water; wipe dry with a cloth. Turn and clean the other side. Re-hang shade and pull down as far as possible to dry completely.

PREPARING WALLS AND WOODWORK
BEFORE PAINTING

1. Wash surfaces to remove dust and dirt and let the surfaces dry thoroughly before painting.
2. If the old paint is partially peeling or flaking, the damaged areas should be sanded smooth before repainting.
3. Always prime bare wood before painting.
4. If the surface to be painted is mildewed, remove the mildew by scrubbing with water and a chlorine bleach.
5. Before painting walls which have previously been wallpapered, first remove the wallpaper and then wash the walls with detergent to remove any paste residue. Allow to dry thoroughly before applying paint.
6. Fill nail holes with toothpaste before repainting walls.

CLEANING WOODWORK

Remove finger smudges on woodwork by rubbing them with kerosene.

PRE-PAINT TEST

Before repainting a wall, do this simple test to determine if the new coat of paint is likely to peel.

Clean a small area, let it dry, then repaint it, allowing it to dry for two days. Next, firmly press a small strip of high quality adhesive tape to the newly-painted area. Jerk the tape off rapidly. If the tape is free of paint, the new paint is well bonded to the old surface. If the new paint adheres to the tape, then the surface must be recleaned and dried before painting.

CEILING TO FLOOR ═══

REMOVING OLD WALLPAPER

Strippable wall coverings may be removed by lifting a corner of the strip and peeling it gently off the wall.

Wallcoverings put up with paste can be removed by three methods:

1. Wet and scrape — First, slit the wallpaper with a knife in a crisscross pattern. Dampen the paper with hot water. After a few minutes, scrape the covering with a putty knife. If the wallpaper has been painted, sand the paint off before trying to remove the paper.
2. Commercial removers — Use the above method substituting commercial wallpaper removers for hot water.
3. Steam removal — If the above two methods fail to remove the wallpaper, rent and use a wallpaper steamer. This method is particularly helpful if there is more than one layer of wallpaper to remove.

CHOOSE PAINT COLORS TO SAVE ENERGY

Dark colors absorb light and will make the room warmer. Light colors reflect light and will make the room cooler. Choose room colors accordingly.

The following chart shows the percentage of light reflected by various colors:

White	80%	Dark Green	9%
Ivory	59%	Pale Green	51%
Peach	53%	Medium Gray	43%
Salmon	53%	Pale Blue	41%
Beige	66%	Deep Rose	12%
Light Ivory	71%		

WOOD PANELING

Clean paneling with a mixture of 1 tablespoon of turpentine, 3 tablespoons of olive oil, and 1 quart of warm water. Wipe dry.

Cooking

COOKING

SAVING MONEY ON MEATS

You can get the most from your meat dollar by learning to estimate the amount needed for your family and by comparing costs per serving. Pieces of a single cut of meat will vary in the amount of fat, gristle, and bone they contain so you will have to decide on the exact amount you will need at the meat counter. Use this guide to help you determine the amounts you need, allowing three ounces as one serving of meat.

One pound of the following cuts will yield 2 to 3 servings:

flank steak
lean stew meats
center cuts of ham
roasts with bones
dressed whole fish
round steak
lean boned roast
veal cutlet
ham
ground meat
liver
fish sticks
poultry

One pound of the following will yield 1 to 2 servings:

rib chops of lamb, pork, or veal
spareribs
T-bone and club steaks
plate and breast of lamb or veal
porterhouse steak
chicken wings and backs

TENDERIZING TOUGH MEATS

Vinegar is a fine tenderizer for tough meats or game. Make a marinade in the proportion of a half cup of vinegar (wine vinegar is good) to a cup of heated liquid, bouillon for instance.

1. Tenderize an inexpensive and perhaps a tough piece of meat by rubbing a little oil and vinegar on both sides and let it stand for two hours before cooking.
2. An old hen can taste like a spring chicken by soaking it in vinegar water for several hours before stewing.

COOKING

KEEPING MEATS FRESH
1. Fresh meats which can't be refrigerated can be preserved temporarily by covering them with salt.
2. If you are unable to cook fresh chicken or ground meat right away, salt the meats immediately. This will prevent spoiling and enables you to keep them a day or two longer before cooking.

MEATS
BROWNING
Salt sprinkled in the pan before browning meat will keep it from sticking.

BROILING
When broiling meats on a rack, place a piece of bread in the broiler pan to soak up the dripping fat. This prevents the fat from smoking and reduces the chances of the fat catching on fire.

BACON AND HAM
COOKING BACON:
Save time by cooking a whole pound of bacon at one time. Separate and place slices on the grid to your broiler pan. Broil 15 minutes, turning once. Then divide it, wrap in foil, and freeze in portions you would use at one time. These servings can be reheated in the oven with no bother and no mess while you are preparing the rest of your breakfast.

P.S. Remember to place a slice of bread in the bottom of the broiler to absorb grease and prevent smoking.

FRYING BACON:
Prevent bacon from curling by:
1. Rinsing in cold water before frying.
2. Sprinkling with flour before frying.

BOILING HAM:
A little vinegar added to water in which you boil ham will remove some of the salty taste and improve the flavor.

STORING FRESH HAMS:
If you are going to store an uncooked ham, rub a little vinegar on the cut end to keep mold from forming.

COOKING

FRYING

HAMBURGERS:
To fry grease-free hamburgers use nothing but a sprinkle of salt on the bottom of your frying pan. Cook over moderate heat.

LIVER:
Liver will shrivel and toughen if salted before frying.

LINK SAUSAGES:
Link sausages will not crack open when frying if first rolled in flour.

SOUPS AND STEWS

1. If soup or stew is too salty, add several slices of raw potato and let it boil five or six minutes. When you remove the potato slices, you remove the excess salt also.
2. A leaf of lettuce dropped into a pot of soup absorbs the grease from the top of the soup. After the lettuce leaf is coated, throw it away.
3. Refrigerate stews or soups until the fat hardens on the top, then remove with a spoon.
4. Add one or two tablespoons of vinegar to beef stews to tenderize the meat.

COOKING WILD GAME

1. Marinate venison, game birds, and other wild game in milk to reduce the "wild" taste.
2. Soak wild game in heavily salted water for 24 hours before cooking or before packaging for freezing.

FISH AND SEAFOOD

TENDER AND FLAVORFUL:
Fish soaked in vinegar and water before cooking will be more tender and have a better flavor.

SLIPPERY FISH:
When preparing something slippery, like fish, wet your hands and then dip them in salt. This helps you get a better grip.

COOKING

FISH AND SEAFOOD (cont.)

COOKING FISH:

Vinegar can be substituted for lemon juice to sprinkle over fish while baking.

COOKING FISH CAKES:

When cooking fish cakes, sprinkle a little salt on the pan to keep the cakes from sticking. This will not add to the salt taste.

CANNED FISH:

1. Vinegar placed in an opened can of sardines or tuna for a few minutes will remove the oily taste.
2. To remove oil from any canned, oily fish, place in a colander and rinse with warm water.

REMOVE "CANNED" TASTE FROM SHRIMP:

To eliminate the "canned" taste from canned shrimp, soak them in a little sherry and two tablespoons of vinegar for about 15 minutes.

TUNA TIPS:

Albacore tuna is the most expensive kind and is prized for its mild flavor and light-colored meat. It is the only tuna labeled "white" on the can. The other three kinds of commercially-sold tuna are labeled "light".

Yellowfin is slightly darker than albacore tuna.

Skipjack and blue fin tuna are darker and oilier than the other varieties.

Packaging:

Solid pack in oil — Light tuna from the fish loin packed in 3 or 4 large pieces. Use for eye-appealing salads.

Chunk-style in oil — Pink or light brown tuna in bite-sized pieces. It's ideal for soups, stews, casseroles, and tossed salads.

Flaked or grated tuna in oil — The cheapest type of all packed in shreds. It works well for sandwich mixtures and dips.

Tuna packed in water — A real calorie savings for dieters. A 3½ ounce portion of water-packed tuna has 109 calories as compared to 155 calories for the same amount of oil-packed tuna.

Low-sodium tuna — Reduced sodium packed tuna contains as little as 95 milligrams per serving.

FISH AND SEAFOOD (cont.)
SCALING FISH:
Before scaling a fish, rub a little vinegar over it to make it less slipppery and easier to handle. The vinegar cuts down on some of the fishy odor on your hands too!
POACHED FISH:
Boiled or poached fish won't crumble so easily if you add a tablespoon of vinegar to the water.
FRYING FISH:
Fish will not curl during frying if placed in the pan skin side down first.
FRYING OYSTERS:
Before frying oysters, place battered oysters on a cookie sheet in the refrigerator for one hour. This will cause the batter to stay on during cooking.

GENERAL HINTS FOR VEGETABLES
WASHING:
Clean vegetables in salted water to remove dirt and other impurities more thoroughly.
COOKING:
A teaspoon of lemon juice or vinegar added to green vegetables will help them retain their color.

BOILING:
Boil vegetables that grow above the ground without a cover, and vegetables that grow below the ground with a cover.
TIRED:
Perk up tired-looking vegetables by soaking them in cold water with 1 or 2 tablespoons of lemon juice.
WILTED:
Perk up slightly wilted vegetables by soaking them face down in ice water to which a teaspoon of vinegar has been added.

COOKING ═══════════════

NUTRITION HINTS

1. Select fresh vegetables over frozen or canned ones whenever possible. Produce fresh from the garden contains the most nutrients. However, frozen or canned foods are better than wrinkled or wilted fresh ones.
2. Store fresh vegetables and fruit as short a time as possible since fewer nutrients are lost with a shorter storage time.
3. Since cooking also destroys some nutrients, cook produce in a small amount of water for a short time in a pan with a tight-fitting lid. Better still, eat vegetables and fruits raw.
4. Steaming vegetables saves more nutrients than when boiling them.
5. Use juices left from cooking vegetables as the liquid in gravies.
6. Cook vegetables in large pieces when possible. This reduces surface area through which water-soluble vitamins can be lost.
7. Store most fruits and vegetables in a cool, dark place since sunlight destroys heat-sensitive vitamins.

DIFFERENT VEGETABLES

CORN:

Salt added to the water when boiling corn or added to fresh creamed corn while cooking toughens it. Salt after removing from heat.

BEAN SPROUTS:

Bean sprouts for salads, sandwiches, or cooking can be grown easily at home. Soak beans overnight in a jar. Pour off water, cover top with cheesecloth or stocking. Put in a dark place with jar placed on side. Each day wet seeds thoroughly, pour off water, return to cabinet. In a few days you will be able to harvest sprouts.

POTATOES:

Soak 20 minutes in hot salty water. Potatoes bake faster.

REMOVE "CANNED" TASTE:

Remove "canned" taste from canned green beans by rinsing in colander before beginning recipe. Add a teaspoon vinegar to canned spinach to enchance the flavor.

DIFFERENT VEGETABLES (cont.)
WASHING AND COOKING CAULIFLOWER:
Soak a head of cauliflower in ice water, flowerets down, before cooking to draw out any hidden insects. Add a teaspoon of vinegar when cooking to prevent discoloration. Be sure to cook with the flowerets down.

DISCOLORED VEGETABLES:
After peeling sweet potatoes, cover them with salt water at once to prevent them from turning dark. Add a little milk to water while cooking cauliflower and add 1 teaspoon lemon juice or vinegar to potatoes as they are cooking to keep them white.

LETTUCE:
Wash lettuce with cold water, dry with paper towels, wrap in a kitchen towel, and refrigerate for 1 hour. Hitting the base of a head of lettuce on the kitchen counter will make it easy to break apart. Breaking lettuce rather than cutting it will prevent the edges from becoming brown and discolored.

CANNING FRUITS AND VEGETABLES
After canning fruits or vegetables, wipe off the outside of the jars after they are filled and sealed with a solution of water and vinegar. This will keep mold from appearing if you have a damp storage area.

PICKLING TIPS
1. Use plain salt only when pickling. Pickles turn dark when iodized salt is used.
2. For delicious pickles, don't use vegetables that have been picked longer than 24 hours.

CRANBERRY SAUCE AND APPLESAUCE
When making cranberry sauce or applesauce, reduce the amount of sugar and add a little salt. This will not only reduce sugar and hence the calories, but will bring out the flavor.

COOKING

CANNING JAM OR JELLY
To prevent a jar of jam or jelly from spoiling, place a cloth soaked in vinegar over the jar before you put the lid on.

JAMS OR JELLIES
A small amount of butter added to the fruit when cooking eliminates the usual foam which forms on the top.

CANDYING APPLES
Fried apples will candy nicely if a little bit of salt is added to the pan.

DISCOLORED FRUIT
Sprinkle lemon juice over sliced apples or bananas to keep them from turning brown.

BITTER GRAPEFRUIT
Salt sprinkled on grapefruit will bring out the natural flavor and reduce any bitter taste.

MILK
HEATING:
Rinse the pot in cold water before heating the milk to keep it from sticking to the bottom.
SOUR:
Slightly soured milk will regain its fresh taste if a pinch of soda is added to it.
FRESH:
A pinch of salt added to fresh milk will keep it sweeter longer.
SCALDING:
Before scalding milk, rinse the pan in cold water to prevent sticking.
SUBSTITUTE BUTTERMILK:
Two teaspoons of vinegar added to one cup of milk will make a good substitute for buttermilk.

BUTTER

Butter can be kept firm without ice by wrapping it in a cloth wrung out in salt water.

EGGS

BEATING:

A little salt added to eggs when you are beating them will speed up the process.

BEATING EGG WHITES:

1. Add a teaspoon of cold water to egg whites while beating to increase the volume.
2. When beating egg whites, don't tap eggbeater on bowl; this causes the whites to lose much of their fluffiness.

BOILING:

Add a little salt to the water in which you boil eggs, and if the eggs crack, the whites will not seep out.

POACHING:

For firmer whites in poached eggs, add either salt or a teaspoon of vinegar to the water in which they are being poached.

PEELING:

1. The eggshells will peel off easier if a teaspoon of salt is added while boiling the eggs.
2. After boiling eggs, plunge them immediately into cold water for 10 or 15 minutes. They will then peel beautifully.

FRYING:

Eggs won't spatter while frying if you sprinkle a little flour on the grease or oil before adding the eggs.

SOUFFLÉS:

Keep soufflés light by adding ¼ teaspoon of cream of tartar to the egg whites during mixing.

OMELET STICKING TO PAN:

Do not salt eggs before beating, this makes them watery. If salted eggs are then whipped for an omelet, this will cause the omelet to stick.

COOKING

EGGS (cont.)

EXPIRATION DATES ON EGGS:

Egg packers can date eggs in two different ways which can be confusing to the buyer. If only the date appears, it refers to the packing date and the eggs can remain in the store for 30 days after that date. If EXP. appears before the date, it refers to the expiration date, and the eggs must be removed from the shelf at that time.

WHIPPING CREAM TIPS

1. If cream seems too thin to whip, first place the dish containing cream in another dish filled with cold water, and then place that dish in a pan of hot water. The cream will then whip without difficulty.
2. Add ¼ teaspoon of lemon juice to whipping cream to make it whip more readily.
3. A pinch of salt added to heavy whipping cream will make it whip faster.

SOUR CREAM SUBSTITUTE

A teaspoon of vinegar blended with one cup of cottage cheese and one-quarter cup of skim milk is a tasty, low-calorie sour cream substitute.

COUNTING CALORIES

1. Cut calories by more than 40% by using nonfat milk in place of whole milk.
2. Eliminate about 20 calories per tablespoon by substituting prepared whipped topping instead of whipped sweetened cream.

CHEESY HINTS

1. To keep cheese fresh and moist, wrap it in a cloth dampened in vinegar and then put it into an air-tight container.
2. Rub butter or margarine over the cut portion of cheese to keep it from drying out.

SLICING CHEESE

A heated knife will enable you to slice cheese thinner.

IRONED SANDWICHES

When traveling, make delicious toasted cheese sandwiches in your motel or hotel room by wrapping them in foil and ironing with a hot iron.

BAKING WITH RAISINS

Raisins coated with flour will not sink to the bottom when added to cake batter.

SPICES AND FLAVORINGS

WATERMELON FLAVOR:

The flavor of watermelon is enhanced by a light sprinkling of salt.

CRUSHED MINT LEAVES:

Freshly chopped or crushed mint leaves will not turn brown during cooking if they are sprinkled with a little vinegar. This will not harm the flavor of the sauce.

SPICES FOR MAIN DISHES:

Spices which can be used for main dishes include bay leaves, chili powder, cumin, curry, marjoram, mustard, oregano, poultry seasoning, red pepper, rosemary, savory, thyme.

ALLSPICE:

The flavor of allspice (whole or ground) is like a blend of cinnamon, nutmeg, and clove.

PARSLEY:

Keep parsley crisp longer by storing in a container with a tight lid. Add salt to fresh parsley before chopping it, and it will chop more easily.

PEELING GARLIC:

For a quick, no-fuss way to peel garlic cloves, simply cut the garlic cloves in half and gently press the knife blade against each half on the peel side. The peeling will come right off.

SLICING MUSHROOMS:

Use an egg slicer to slice mushrooms.

ONION RINGS:

Soak raw onion rings in ice water for one hour before battering and frying. They are crisper and more delicious this way.

COOKING

MAYONNAISE OR CATSUP (Last Drop)
To get the last little bit of mayonnaise or catsup out of the jar or bottle, dribble a little vinegar into the jar, put the top on tightly and shake.

PASTAS AND RICE
BOILING:
Add 1 to 2 tablespoons of oil to the water when cooking pastas to prevent them from boiling over.
GOOEY RICE:
One tablespoon of butter or oil added to the water before adding the rice will prevent rice from becoming gooey or sticking to the pan.
WHITE, FLUFFY RICE:
Add ½ teaspoon of lemon juice to rice as it cooks to make it whiter and fluffier.

PANCAKES
Rub a slice of raw potato over the griddle before cooking pancakes to keep them from sticking.

CREAMY GRITS
For extra creamy, Southern-style grits, stir a little milk into the pot just before serving the grits. Delicious.

LIMP CEREAL, POTATO CHIPS, COOKIES, AND CRACKERS
To rejuvenate limp cereal, potato chips, cookies, or crackers, place these items on a cookie sheet in a moderate oven for a few minutes. Return to package and close tightly.

FLUFFY POPCORN
For fluffy popcorn, store unpopped corn in the freezer.

REFRESHING STALE ROLLS
Sprinkle stale rolls, muffins, or biscuits with water, place in a brown bag or foil, and heat in a slow oven for 15 minutes. They will taste freshly baked.

SUBSTITUTIONS FOR WHEAT

If you are allergic to wheat, you can substitute these flours for 1 cup of wheat flour:

1 cup of barley flour
1 cup of corn flour
3/4 cup of coarse cornmeal
1 cup of fine cornmeal
7/8 cup of rice flour
1-1/4 cups of rye flour

1-1/3 cups of oat flour
5/8 cup of potato starch flour

SHINY BREAD CRUST

You will get a nice shiny top on your homemade bread if you brush it with vinegar the last few minutes of baking.

CAKES AND FROSTINGS

SMOOTH CAKE BATTER:

For a smoother cake batter
1. Add 2 or 3 tablespoons of milk while creaming the sugar and butter.
2. Add 2 tablespoons of boiling water when creaming the sugar and eggs. This trick makes a wonderful difference.

REMOVING CAKES FROM PANS:

For easy removal of cake layers, place the pans on a damp cloth immediately after taking the pans from the oven.

BUNNY CAKE:

1. You'll need a 9" square cake for this bunny. Use any treasured recipe or cake mix baked as directed. When the cake is cool, cut two 1½" strips from one side of cake for bunny ears. The large cake piece is the bunny's face.
2. Arrange the cake pieces on a tray. Then spread a fluffy white, seven minute frosting over top and sides of bunny's face and ears — make it nice and swirly.
3. Now with coconut give your bunny lots of soft snowy-white fur. If you wish, tint a little of the coconut pink to put inside the ears. Use shiny jelly beans for eyes, nose, and mouth...pink pipe cleaners for whiskers...and licorice sticks for a bow tie.

COOKING ════════════════

CAKES AND FROSTINGS (cont.)
FROSTING CAKES:
1. To make frosting cakes easier, dip your knife in hot water frequently.
2. Prevent icing from running off a cake by dusting the surface with cornstarch before icing.

NUTS
NUTS IN CAKES:
Nuts will not settle to the bottom of cake batter if they are first heated in the oven and then dusted with flour before adding to the batter.

SHELLING PECANS:
You won't have any trouble shelling pecans if they are first soaked in boiling water for 10 or 15 minutes.

PECANS AND WALNUTS:
Pecans and walnuts can be easily removed from their shells if you soak them overnight in salt water.

PIES
COOKING JUICY PIES:
To prevent juices from cooking out of pies into the oven, place a four inch piece of uncooked macaroni upright in the center of the pie.

PECAN OR MAPLE SYRUP PIES:
A teaspoon of vinegar added to pecan pie or maple syrup pie will cut the sugary sweetness and bring out the flavor.

FLUFFY MERINGUES:
Meringues will be unusually fluffy if you add one-fourth of a teaspoon of vinegar to three egg whites.

CRISP PIE CRUST:
For a nice crisp pie crust or the perfect crust on bread or rolls, make the dough by substituting one tablespoon of vinegar for one of the tablespoons of ice water.

PREVENTING STICKING:
Place pie with a crumb crust on a hot wet towel a few minutes before serving to keep the crust from sticking to the pie pan.

COOKIES AND CANDIES
BAKING COOKIES:
1. Cookies will not spread more than they should if they are placed on cool baking sheets before baking.
2. Dust greased cookie sheets with a little flour. This will keep the cookies from spreading during baking.

KEEPING COOKIES SOFT:
Cookies will remain soft and fresh if a slice of bread is stored with them in the cookie jar.

BOILED ICING OR CANDY:
Boiled icing or candy can be prevented from becoming sugary if you add a little vinegar to the ingredients before cooking. Candy will not boil over the pot if the edge is coated with butter.

TOO SWEET CANDY:
When cooking candy, if it seems too sweet, add a pinch of salt.

CHOCOLATE SLIVERS:
Make chocolate slivers by grating the chocolate with a potato peeler.

MELTING CHOCOLATE:
When melting chocolate, form a cup from aluminum foil. The chocolate will slide off the foil easily, and there is no messy pan to clean.

CHOPPING MARSHMALLOWS:
Dip your knife or kitchen shears in hot water frequently when chopping marshmallows to keep them from sticking to the utensil.

MARSHMALLOW CREAM:
Before removing marshmallow cream from jar run hot water over spoon — or run hot water over the jar before taking top off.

BROWN SUGAR
A wedge of apple, lemon, or orange placed with hardened brown sugar in a tightly-closed jar will soften the sugar. To keep brown sugar soft, place it in an air-tight container with a slice of fresh bread. If the sugar is already hard when purchased, the bread will soften it in two days.

COOKING ══════════════════

COOLING PUDDING
Cool hot pudding quickly by placing the dish in cold salt water.

FIRM GELATIN SALAD
A teaspoon of vinegar added to any gelatin recipe will keep molded salads or desserts from melting away before your eyes.

CONGEALING GELATIN
1. When making congealed salads, bring the gelatin and hot water to a rolling boil before placing it to cool. This keeps it from melting so quickly when you are ready to use it.
2. If you place a gelatin mold in water to cool, a little salt and baking soda added to the water will cause the gelatin to set more quickly.

PEELING, OPENING, AND CHOPPING
PEELING ORANGES:
Place oranges in a hot oven for 2 or 3 minutes before peeling, and no white fiber will be left on the orange.

PEELING ORANGES AND GRAPEFRUIT:
To peel oranges or grapefruit and free fruit entirely from the membranous or white pulp underneath the skin, place the fruit in hot water for five minutes before peeling. You will then be able to peel every particle of membrane from the pulp.

PEELING TOMATOES AND PEACHES:
Dip tomatoes and peaches in boiling water for 1 minute for easy peeling.

OPENING COCONUTS:
Coconuts are easier to open if placed in a preheated oven at 325° for 15 minutes before cracking.

CHOPPING DATES:
Dip your knife or kitchen shears in hot water frequently when chopping dates to keep them from sticking to the utensil.

COOKING

FOOD ODORS
FOODS WITH STRONG ODORS:
While cooking foods with a strong odor, put a cupful of vinegar on the stove or put the heel of a loaf of bread on top of cabbage, broccoli, or brussels sprouts.

BOILING CABBAGE OR BEETS:
A little vinegar added to the water in which you boil cabbage or beets will help the vegetables to retain their natural colors as well as cut down the cooking odors.

CABBAGE ODORS:
Cook cabbage with a whole walnut to eliminate cabbage odor while cooking.

PREVENTING STICKING
1. Vinegar brought to a boil in a new frying pan will help season the pan and prevent foods from sticking in the future.
2. When pan frying or sautéing, always heat your pan before adding the butter or oil. Not even eggs stick when using this method.
3. If muffins are stuck to the pan, place the hot pan on a wet towel. They will then slide right out.
4. Sprinkle a little salt into the frying pan to prevent splattering.

DEEP FAT FRYING
When deep fat frying, add a tablespoon of vinegar to the fat (before it is heated) to keep the food from absorbing too much fat and to eliminate the greasy taste.

USING A DOUBLE BOILER
When using a double boiler, put some salt in the bottom pot, and food will cook faster. Keep a careful eye on icings to prevent scorching.

CHAFING DISH HINTS
1. Only wooden utensils or fine wire whisks should be used in your chafing dish. Other utensils might scratch the dish's finish.
2. Do not overheat. Use heat sparingly.

COOKING

BOILING WATER QUICKLY

Add salt to water you are boiling to hasten the process.

FREEZER-STORED FOODS

1. For the best taste and appearance, package foods properly by wrapping them in aluminum foil, plastic boxes, plastic bags, or in laminated freezer paper.
2. To prevent food from becoming stale, the entire contents of your freezer should be eaten within the course of the year.
3. Since spices will become stronger in the freezer, use half the amount of spices called for in cakes or casseroles which you plan to freeze.

MEASURING SHORTENING

Shortening will come out of a measuring cup readily if eggs have been beaten or measured in the cup beforehand.

MEASURING SYRUP AND HONEY

Every drop of syrup and honey will come right out of the measurer if the cup or spoon is first rubbed with oleo.

FOODS TOO SALTY

If food is too salty, correct this problem by adding one teaspoon sugar mixed with one tablespoon of vinegar to it.

LUMPY GRAVY

To prevent lumps from forming when making gravy or thickening stews, mix the flour or cornstarch with a little salted hot water.

FRESH COFFEE

Coffee stored in the refrigerator or freezer will retain its fresh flavor.

LEFT-OVERS

Keep a plastic container with a tight-fitting lid in the freezer ready to store any small amount of left-overs. Include meat as well as vegetables. When the container is full, add a little water or other liquid, simmer for an hour, and enjoy a hearty "free" soup.

Furniture and Accessories

FURNITURE AND ACCESSORIES

ADHESIVES
BRASS
CANDLE WAX
CERAMIC WARE
CHINA
CHROME FURNITURE
COPPER
CRYSTAL
CUTGLASS
DUSTING
EBONY
FIGURINES
LAMPSHADES
LEATHER
MARBLE
PEWTER
PIANOS
STAINLESS STEEL FLATWARE
STERLING SILVER FLATWARE
TELEPHONES
UPHOLSTERY
VASES
VINYL UPHOLSTERY
WICKER
WOOD FURNITURE

FURNITURE AND
ACCESSORIES

CLEANING WOOD FURNITURE

Clean wood surfaces by using any one of the following methods:

1. Wash the wood with warm water and a mild soap. After scrubbing gently, wipe clean with a damp cloth. Rub dry with a soft cloth.
2. Wipe the wood with a cloth dampened with water and vinegar.
3. Rub the wood with a hot damp cloth that has been dipped in furniture oil. Follow by rubbing with a soft dry cloth.
4. Apply a good application of mineral spirits with a soft cloth. Let it set for 5 minutes. If the wood has a heavy wax build-up, repeat the procedure.

WHITE RINGS ON WOOD FURNITURE

There are several methods of treating white rings on wood. Use any one of the following methods and follow the treatment by polishing with furniture wax, floor wax, or your favorite polish. You can rub the ring with:

1. Cigarette ashes
2. Toothpaste
3. Salad oil
4. Linseed oil
5. Turpentine
6. Rubbing alcohol — Rub ring quickly, then dry with a soft cloth.
7. Mayonnaise — Leave on 1 to 2 hours before wiping off.

Be sure to polish the furniture after treating it.

PREVENTING WATER MARKS ON TABLES

White water marks can be prevented from marring your tables by waxing them with floor wax. Apply the wax with a soft cloth and rub in immediately. This leaves a water resistant finish on furniture.

PREVENTING FURNITURE SCRATCHES

Glue felt to the bottoms of vases, ashtrays, and figurines to prevent these accessories from scratching furniture surfaces.

FURNITURE AND ACCESSORIES

REMOVING SCRATCHES FROM WOOD FURNITURE

1. Scratches can be filled on light or dark wood by rubbing them with camphor oil. Apply with a soft cloth and rub in the direction of the grain of the wood. The darker the wood, the more oil you need to apply. Camphor oil can be bought at drugstores.
2. Fill scratches on walnut wood by rubbing the meat of a walnut into the scratch.
3. Fill scratches on cherry or mahogany by applying iodine with a cotton swab or a toothpick.
4. Scratches can be removed by rubbing with liquid or paste shoe polish.

REMOVING CIGARETTE BURNS ON WOOD

With a small knife, gently scrape away all the discoloration in the damaged area. When the discoloration has been removed, apply clear fingernail polish and let it harden. Repeat this until the cavity is filled completely level.

ALCOHOL SPOTS ON WOOD FURNITURE

1. Rub spot with paste wax or paste silver polish. After spot is removed, polish surface as usual.
2. Rub spot quickly with a damp cloth dipped in ammonia. Polish as usual after spot is removed.

REMOVING ADHESIVE LABELS FROM WOOD FURNITURE

Price tag stickers or adhesive labels used when moving or when placing your furniture in storage can damage the wood finish. Remove the sticker as soon as possible to prevent it from bonding to the wood. If you are unable to remove all of the paper or adhesive, scrub the remainder with a washcloth dipped in cooking oil until the spot is removed.

FURNITURE AND
ACCESSORIES

CANDLE WAX ON WOOD SURFACES

Remove candle wax on wood surfaces by first hardening the wax with an ice cube, and then removing as much of the wax as possible with a table knife. Rub the spot with liquid wax, then wipe dry. Repeat until spot is removed.

PAINT SPLATTERS ON FURNITURE

To remove fresh water-based paint, rub with a cloth dampened in water. To remove fresh oil-based paint, rub gently with fine steel wool dipped in paste wax. To remove dried paint, saturate the spot with boiled linseed oil and let stand for awhile. Wipe the area and remove any remaining paint with a paste made of pumice powder and mineral oil.

WASHING UPHOLSTERY

Upholstery with a hard finish can be washed with a sponge dipped in the suds of a mild detergent and water. Use a circular motion, overlapping the areas. Work on one area at a time, wiping each washed section with a terry cloth towel dampened with clear water.

NOTE: Before washing, vacuum the upholstery thoroughly to remove as much dust and dirt as possible.

CLEANING VINYL UPHOLSTERY

Wash vinyl with mild detergent and water using a sponge. Rinse with clear water and dry with a towel.

NOTE: Since body oils cause vinyl to become stiff and crack, it is necessary to wash vinyl head and arm rests more frequently.

CLEANING WICKER

Clean wicker once a year. First, scrub it gently with a brush and mild detergent and water. After washing, rinse it thoroughly with the garden hose and let it air dry. When the wicker dries completely, it can be repainted.

REMOVING RUST ON CHROME FURNITURE

Scrub rust spots with steel wool no. 0000 dipped in kerosene. When all spots are removed, apply a sealer.

FURNITURE AND ACCESSORIES

MOVING HEAVY FURNITURE

Heavy furniture can be moved across wood, asphalt, linoleum, or brick floors easily and without marring the floors by slipping small rugs or bathmats under the two back legs. After the mats are in place, tilt the furniture on its back legs and slide to the new location.

CAUTION: Make sure the rugs are very thick.

CLEANING EBONY

Clean ebony with dark red furniture oil applied with a damp cloth. Rub with a soft, dry cloth after applying the oil. You always oil ebony, never wax it.

CLEANING BRASS

Brass can be cleaned and the tarnish removed by either of the following methods:
1. Rub with very fine steel wool and ammonia.
2. Rub with half of a lemon dipped in salt.
3. Rub with a mixture of rottenstone powder and linseed oil.
4. Rub with a paste made with 2 tablespoons of salt, 1 cup of vinegar, and enough flour to form a paste.

After the brass is clean, wash well with hot water and a mild detergent. Rinse well and dry with a soft cloth.

PEWTER CARE

1. Keep pewter looking good by washing it regularly with soapsuds and hot water. Rinse thoroughly to avoid leaving any soap film.
2. Tarnish can be removed from antique pewter with no. 0000 steel wool dipped in olive oil. (The olive oil keeps the steel wool from scratching the pewter.) After removing the tarnish, wash the pewter and rinse thoroughly before drying with a soft cloth.
3. New pewter can be cleaned with ammonia and a soft cloth. After cleaning, wash and rinse thoroughly before drying with a soft cloth.

CAUTION: Never use acids on pewter or wash in an automatic dishwasher.

FURNITURE AND
ACCESSORIES

PROTECTING BRASS

Clean, untarnished brass can be sprayed with a clear lacquer for a lasting finish or rubbed with a cloth lightly moistened with olive oil to prevent it from tarnishing.

MARBLE CARE

1. Dust marble with a soft dry cloth or wipe with a damp cloth as frequently as you would any other accessory or piece of furniture.
2. Twice a year wash the marble with a mild detergent to prevent it from becoming dull.
3. Treat organic stains, such as coffee or tea, by placing white paper towels saturated with hydrogen peroxide and a few drops of household ammonia on the stain. Cover the towels with a sheet of plastic or a flat pyrex dish to hold the moisture in the towels. Keep the moist towels on the stains until they are removed. This procedure may take several hours. After the marble is cleaned, rinsed, and dried, polish with a non-yellowing wax.
4. Remove ink stains by placing white paper towels saturated with rubbing alcohol on the stain for 1 hour. Follow this by placing paper towels saturated with household ammonia for 1 hour on the spot. Finally, place paper towels soaked in hydrogen peroxide on the stain. When the spot is removed, rinse marble, dry, and polish with a non-yellowing wax.
5. Oil and grease stains can be removed by placing white paper towels saturated with mineral spirits on the stain until it is removed. Cover the towels with a sheet of plastic or place a pyrex dish on them to hold the moisture in the towels. When the stain is removed, bleach with hydrogen peroxide, wash with mild detergent and water, rinse, dry, and polish with a non-yellowing wax.

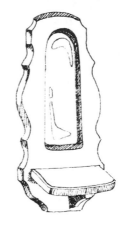

FURNITURE AND ACCESSORIES

CLEANING COPPER

Clean badly-tarnished copper without any effort with this method:

1. Wash the piece with detergent and water to remove dust and grease.
2. Apply a mixture of the juice of 1 lemon and 1 teaspoon of salt. Leave this solution on the copper piece for 30 minutes.
3. Rub the copper gently with no. 0000 steel wool until the tarnish has been removed.

   CAUTION: Don't overclean old copper. Leave some shading around handles, spouts, and dents.
4. Wash thoroughly with detergent and water to remove all traces of the salt and lemon juice. Rinse well. If salt and lemon juice are not removed completely, the copper will turn green.
5. For a more lasting protection, spray cleaned copper with 1 coat of clear lacquer after first wiping it with denatured alcohol. Allow the piece to dry completely before applying lacquer. After spraying the copper, let it dry at least 1 hour.
6. For daily or weekly cleaning for uncoated copper, clean with a mixture of half toothpaste and half baking soda. Wash and dry thoroughly.
7. For daily or weekly cleaning for coated copper, clean with lemon oil. Rub with a soft cloth after cleaning.

VASES

Prevent fragile vases from getting turned over when dusting or arranging by filling them with sand.

ROUGH EDGES ON CRYSTAL

Crystal goblets with rough edges or small chips can be repaired at home. Rub the edge gently with emery cloth until the rim is smooth again.

CHINA WITH GOLD OR PLATINUM BANDS

Gold or platinum bands on fine china may smear if wiped while still hot after washing and rinsing in hot water.

FURNITURE AND
ACCESSORIES

WASHING GLASS VASES, BOWLS, CRYSTAL, AND CLOUDY CUTGLASS

1. Temperature changes can cause glassware to crack, so always have the water you rinse glassware in the same temperature as the wash water.
2. To avoid breakage, crystal should not be washed in the dishwasher.
3. Cloudy cutglass can usually be restored to its original brilliance by soaking it in a solution of water and toilet bowl crystals. Use a baby bottle brush to scrub inside narrow vases, decanters, or pitchers. This may take several days, but it is worth the effort.
   CAUTION: Wear rubber gloves when using toilet bowl crystals.

STAINLESS STEEL FLATWARE WARNING

If you should ever wash your sterling silver in the dishwasher, make sure you do not wash stainless steel in the washer basket at the same time. This would damage the stainless. This sounds backwards, but it's true.

CLEANING STERLING SILVER FLATWARE

Wash your sterling silver flatware by hand in warm, sudsy water to save the beautiful patina of lovely silver. Dishwashing detergent tends to add a high sheen to the silver as well as removing the darkened, oxidized indentions.

METALLIC MARKS ON CERAMIC WARE

Metallic-looking marks which appear on ceramic ware probably are caused by something metal rubbing against it in the dishwasher. These marks can be removed by rubbing them gently with steel wool.

DUSTING

1. Keep up with your dusting the easy way by dusting at odd moments. You can dust when you are waiting for guests to arrive or while waiting for activities to begin. This gets the job done without taking a big block of time.
2. Dust books easily with a wide paintbrush.

FURNITURE AND ACCESSORIES

WEIGHTED FIGURINES
Hollow figurines with an opening at the bottom can be weighted by filling with melted candles or paraffin. This makes them less fragile and less likely to be broken.

LAMP SHADES
If the humidity has caused cloth lamp shades to look loose and rippled, turn on the lamp and let the heat from the light bulb dry out the fabric.

POLISHING LEATHER TABLE TOPS
Use saddlesoap to polish leather table tops. After applying the saddlesoap with a soft cloth, let it remain on the leather for about 30 minutes. After that length of time, brush vigorously, then buff with a cloth for shine.

CLEANING PIANOS AND PIANO KEYS
1. Plastic keys can be cleaned with a cloth dampened with water and wrung very dry. Rub immediately afterwards with a soft, dry cloth.
2. Ivory keys can be cleaned with a cloth dampened with milk, followed with a cloth dampened with water. Wring these cloths very dry. Rub immediately afterwards with a soft, dry cloth.
3. Really dirty piano keys can be cleaned with toothpaste and an old, soft toothbrush. Remove toothpaste with a cloth dampened with water and wrung dry. Rub immediately afterwards with a soft, dry cloth.

   CAUTION: Keep all moisture from going down between keys. Always work quickly when using damp cloths and always follow immediately with dry cloths.
4. For in-between major cleaning, dust the piano keys frequently with a soft, dry cloth.
5. Give your keyboard a chance to "breathe" by leaving the keyboard lid up during normal circumstances. This helps prevent the keys from turning yellow.
6. The inside of a grand piano can be vacuumed gently with the brush attachment of the vacuum cleaner.

CLEANING TELEPHONE DIALS
Telephone dials can be cleaned easily with a cotton swab dipped in a solution of vinegar and water.

Kitchen Cleaning

KITCHEN CLEANING

APPLIANCES
BREADBOXES
BROILER PAN AND GRID
COUNTERS
CRYSTAL AND GLASSWARE
DISHES
FREEZER
GARBAGE BAGS
GARBAGE DISPOSALS
IRON COOKWARE
JARS
LUNCHBOXES
NONSTICK SURFACES
ODORS
OVENS
PERCOLATORS
PLACEMATS
POTS AND PANS
REFRIGERATOR
ROACHES AND WEEVILS
TEAKETTLES
WOODEN SALAD BOWLS

KITCHEN CLEANING

KITCHEN COUNTERS

Kitchen counters can be cleaned without marring by using soda as the cleaning agent.

OILING KITCHEN APPLIANCES

Oil your kitchen appliances as you cook by putting a few drops of vegetable oil on the movable parts of the mixer, blender, or food processor.

CLEANING APPLIANCES

Remove grease and grime from appliances by scrubbing with undiluted vinegar.

CLEANING PERCOLATORS

Perk 1 or 2 tablespoons of powdered laundry or dishwasher detergent in your percolator. This cleans the pot effectively and effortlessly. Do this about once a week. Make sure you rinse the pot well after cleaning to avoid giving your coffee a soapy taste.

CLEANING THE REFRIGERATOR

Soda is excellent for cleaning the inside of the refrigerator. It will not only clean without scratching, but will remove odors as well.

CLEANING FREEZERS

1. Use a solution of 2 tablespoons of baking soda to 1 quart of warm water to clean the interior of a freezer. Clean a frost-free model once a year and a manual defrost model whenever the frost builds up to ¼ inch thick.
2. Keep the freezer odorless by putting an opened box of baking soda in it. This will remove all stale odors.

KITCHEN CLEANING

SELF-CLEANING OVENS

A self-cleaning oven is more economical to operate than a manual one. Because of the extra insulation required for self-cleaning ovens, heat is retained longer. To take advantage of existing heat, clean the oven immediately after using it for baking or roasting.

OVEN GREASE

To prevent grease from building up in the oven, wipe it with a sponge or cloth dampened in vinegar.

MINI GARBAGE BAGS

Save bread bags and vegetable bags to be used as mini garbage bags. This is especially good for bones or wet garbage.

GARBAGE DISPOSALS

1. Garbage disposals should be run using cold water. This solidifies the grease, helping it wash out without clogging the drain.
2. After disposal is cleaned, grind citrus peelings, using hot water, to give your kitchen a fresh, pleasing smell.

PEANUT BUTTER AND MAYONNAISE JARS

Rinse old peanut butter or mayonnaise jars with vinegar before reusing them. This eliminates the odor of the former contents.

CLOUDY GLASSWARE

To make cloudy glassware sparkle, rub the glasses with newspapers and a paste made with salt and water.

KITCHEN CLEANING

WASHING GLASSWARE BY HAND

When washing dishes by hand, eliminate soap film on glassware by adding a little vinegar to the rinse water.

GREASY, SMELLY PANS AND DISHES

When washing very greasy or smelly pans or dishes, put a few tablespoons of vinegar in the dishwasher to cut down the grease and to help remove the odor.

SEASONING NEW IRON COOKWARE

Cast iron cookware can be seasoned by rubbing it with a thin coat of solid, unsalted shortening and baking it several hours in a 200° oven before using. Repeat this procedure after the first few times of use. Do not use liquid shortening.

STAINS ON NONSTICK COOKING SURFACES
(Silverstone and Teflon)

These surfaces can be stained from minerals in water, baked-on fat, or the use of excessive heat. Each of the following formulas is effective in removing these stains.
1. ¼ cup coffee pot cleaner in 1 quart of water
2. 3 tablespoons oxygen bleach and 1 teaspoon of mild dishwashing detergent mixed with 1 cup of water
3. 3 tablespoons dishwasher detergent in 1 cup of water

Let the solution simmer in the stained pan for 15 to 20 minutes. After this treatment, wash the pan thoroughly, rinse, and dry. Recondition the pan with cooking oil or shortening before using.

BROILER PAN AND GRID

Make cleaning a broiler pan and grid much easier with this procedure:

While the pan is still hot, pour off drippings, fill it with hot water, replace grid. Sprinkle grid generously with detergent and cover with wet paper towels. Put pan back into the warm oven for about 20 minutes. The heat will help loosen grease and burned-on particles. Any stubborn stains can be removed with steel wool.

KITCHEN CLEANING

OATMEAL POT

For easier, quicker cleaning, soak the pot in which you have cooked oatmeal in cold water rather than hot water.

BURNED-ON FOOD ON OVENWARE

Badly burned-on food can be removed from small glass ovenware containers by placing them in a slow cooker filled with water and ½ cup of baking soda and a little vinegar. Cook on high for 3 or 4 hours. When you remove the dish, it will be like new.

LIME DEPOSITS IN TEAKETTLES

Lime deposits can be removed from your teakettle by heating vinegar in it and letting it stand overnight. Rinse the next day.

LUNCHBOXES AND BREADBOXES

1. Wash lunchboxes and breadboxes with a vinegar-water solution to prevent mold from forming.
2. A piece of fresh bread dampened with vinegar left in lunchboxes and breadboxes will rid them of their stale odor.

ALUMINUM UTENSIL STAINS

1. Stains and discolorations can be removed from aluminum by boiling with a solution of 2 to 3 tablespoons of cream of tartar, lemon juice, or vinegar to each quart of water.
2. Stubborn stains can be removed by rubbing with fine steel wool.

CRACKED DISHES

When you crack a favorite dish or plate, put it in a pan of milk and boil it for 45 minutes. Not only will the crack usually disappear, but the dish actually becomes stronger.

KITCHEN CLEANING

KITCHEN PLACEMATS
Apply a thin coat of liquid wax to textured, dull-finished placemats to keep them from absorbing stains from coffee, tea, or other foods.

STRAW PLACEMATS
Revitalize warped straw placemats by immersing them in hot sudsy water. Rinse, blot between paper towels, and weight down under some heavy objects for a day. The mats will dry flat and be as good as new.

CARE OF WOODEN SALAD BOWLS
Wooden salad bowls should be rinsed and dried immediately, not washed or soaked. Periodically revitalize the bowls by rubbing with vegetable oil inside and out. Let oil soak in overnight, removing any excess oil with paper towels next day.

KITCHEN ODORS
Rid the kitchen of offensive odors or prevent them from forming by:
1. Pouring hot salt water down the drain once or twice a week.
2. Grinding citrus peelings or apple cores in the garbage disposal.
3. Boiling water in an uncovered pan which has a few cloves added to it.
4. Boiling vinegar in an uncovered pan or keeping a small uncovered container of vinegar in the corner of your kitchen counter.

REFRIGERATOR ODORS
Unpleasant refrigerator odors can be eliminated by:
1. Placing a cotton ball saturated with vanilla, lemon, or peppermint extract in the refrigerator.
2. Keeping an opened box of soda on a refrigerator shelf.
3. Keeping 3 or 4 pieces of charcoal on the refrigerator door shelf.

KITCHEN CLEANING

FOOD ODORS ON HANDS

Rid your hands of garlic or onion odors by washing them with a mixture of soda and water or by rubbing them with lemon juice.

ROACH CONTROL

These are effective insecticides against roaches.

1. Put baking soda or boric acid in dark kitchen cabinets, under the sink, or any other spots that roaches might frequent.
2. Place bay leaves in kitchen cabinets or drawers.

WEEVILS IN KITCHEN CABINETS

Bay leaves placed in kitchen cabinets and drawers will keep away weevils as well as roaches.

Laundry

LAUNDRY

COLLARS AND CUFFS
CORDUROY
DAMPENED CLOTHES
DIAPERS
DINGY CLOTHES
DOWN VESTS AND JACKETS
FIBERGLASS CURTAINS
FOAM RUBBER
IRONING
LEATHER AND VINYL
LINEN
MARKING CLOTHES
NYLON CURTAINS
PILLOWS
PRESS CLOTHS
SILK
STARCHING
STOCKINGS
SUEDE
TIMESAVER TIPS
VELVET
VELVETEEN
WOOL

LAUNDRY

NOTE:

For information on how to treat specific spots and stains, see the section called SPOTS AND STAINS on page 103.

LAUNDRY TIME SAVERS

1. Save ironing time by keeping a rack for hanging clothes adjacent to the dryer. When the no-iron clothes have finished drying, hang them up immediately so that no ironing touch-ups are necessary. Be sure to button the top button of shirts to keep the collars in place.
2. Save time in sorting and folding socks by placing a large basket next to the dryer and keeping all of the clean socks in it. Let each person pick up his own socks.
3. Save time in sorting the laundry by having 3 laundry hampers and labeling them "white", "colored", and "delicate." Let each member of the family sort his own dirty laundry.

STEAMING WRINKLED VELVET

Hang velvet garments in the bathroom and turn the hot water on until the bathroom is thick with steam. Let the velvet steam for 30 minutes, then brush. The wrinkles will fall out.

WASHING DIAPERS

Soak in cold water with a mild detergent or soap powder for several hours, or overnight, before washing. Wash in hot water with more detergent or soap powder. If a chlorine bleach is used, wash thoroughly after diapers are bleached to prevent a diaper rash due to the chlorine.

WASHING DINGY, GREY, OR YELLOWED CLOTHES

Soak the clothes in hot water with twice the amount of detergent usually used. Soak several hours. Rewash in hot water with a chlorine bleach.

LAUNDRY

WASHING COLLARS AND CUFFS

1. Rub liquid detergent or a paste made from powdered detergent and water into the soiled areas. Brush these treated areas with a nail brush. Let stand for 1 hour before washing.
2. Add two or three terry cloth towels to a machine load of shirts. Turn the shirts inside out and let the towels scrub the necks and cuffs during the wash cycle.

FABRIC WHITENERS

A teaspoon of borax into the last water in which the clothes are rinsed will whiten them surprisingly. Pound the borax so it will dissolve easily.

CLEANING LEATHER AND VINYL

Clean leather and vinyl by rubbing gently with a cloth dampened with water and mild detergent. Rinse with a cloth dampened with clear water. Rub dry with a clean cloth.

NOTE: For other hints on leather care see page 124.

FIBERGLASS CURTAINS

Fiberglass curtains should be handwashed and drip-dried unless the manufacturer recommends machine washing. Rubbing can cause holes to form or the fabric to become frayed, so handle soiled areas gently.

SILK, SUEDE, LINEN

Never treat pure silk, suede, or 100% linen at home. Always take garments made from these materials to a professional dry cleaners.

NYLON CURTAINS

To make your nylon curtains look like new, add 1 cup Epsom salts to 1 gallon of water when rinsing.

FOAM RUBBER

Do not dry foam rubber in the dryer. This causes the rubber to crumble.

LAUNDRY

DRYING DOWN VESTS AND JACKETS
After washing down garments, place them with a tennis shoe in the dryer to reduce static cling.

COLORFAST STOCKINGS
Add vinegar to the rinse water to set the color.

HURRY-UP DRYING FOR STOCKINGS
To dry stockings in a hurry, place the freshly-washed stockings on a large bath towel, roll the stockings in the towel, wring, unroll, and hang stockings on a towel rack. They dry quickly this way.

DRIP DRYING CLOTHES
Place a spring expansion shower curtain rod lengthwise over the center of the tub and use it for all drip drying. It is convenient for clothes on hangers as well as for curtains, spreads, and blankets.

PERSPIRATION ODOR IN WOOLENS
Remove perspiration odor in woolens by soaking them in a solution of 4 tablespoons of salt and 1 quart of cold water before washing as usual.

PRESS CLOTHS
A baby diaper makes a wonderful press cloth.

SMOOTH IRONING
1. To help the iron glide smoothly over fabrics, keep the soleplate clean. Scour the soleplate with a damp sponge sprinkled with baking soda. Scrub gently. The soda is a gentle abrasive which will not scratch or dull surfaces.
2. Rubbing a hot iron over a piece of paraffin or a candle will make the soleplate smooth and the ironing easier. Be sure to iron over a piece of scrap cloth before pressing your garments in order to absorb any excess wax.

LAUNDRY

PRESSING VELVETEEN AND CORDUROY
Never put the weight of the iron on these fabrics. This includes a steam iron. Instead, place a damp cloth on the fabric and press gently using the steam control on your iron.

DAMPENED CLOTHES
Place dampened clothes in a plastic bag in the refrigerator if you plan on ironing them within 48 hours. Place them in the freezer if you won't be able to iron them for awhile. This is especially convenient for napkins and placemats since you can pull them out and iron them as needed.

CAUTION: Wrap colored clothes and white clothes separately.

STARCHING
When using spray starch on dark-colored clothes, spray on the wrong side to prevent white streaks from the starch from showing.

MARKING CLOTHES FOR LAUNDERING
Here is an easy and permanent method of marking clothes for campers, students, scouts, and athletes.
1. Use a wide, black, felt pen. Make sure it is permanent ink.
2. *On teeshirts and undershirts:* Write the name on the inside of the bottom hem. It won't show through.
3. *On jeans or slacks:* Write the name on the inside pocket.
4. *On underpants and gym shorts:* Stretch the waistband and write the name on the stretched elastic. When it snaps back, it can be read easily.
5. *On dresses, shirts, blouses, jackets:* Write initials or last name on the labels.

FRESHENING PILLOWS
Spray pillows with a disinfectant and dry in the dryer for 30 minutes.

Personal Grooming

PERSONAL GROOMING

BODY
BURNS
CONDITIONERS
CLEANSER
EYES
FACE
FEET
HAIR
HANDS
MOUTH
NAILS
SKIN

═══════PERSONAL GROOMING

FRUIT STAINS ON HANDS

Remove fruit or berry stains from your hands by using one of the following methods:
1. Rinsing with lemon juice
2. Rinsing with vinegar
3. Rubbing stubborn stains with salt and lemon juice

FELT MARKER STAINS ON HANDS

Stains on your hands caused by felt markers can be removed by spraying the skin with hairspray, then wiping off. The marks come off immediately.

SKIN CLEANSER

An excellent, slightly abrasive skin cleanser is cornmeal. Lather your hands with mild soap, sprinkle the meal into the suds and gently rub your face and neck. This cleans the pores and leaves the skin clean and revitalized.

FOOD ODORS ON HANDS

Rid your hands of garlic or onion odors by washing them with a mixture of soda and water or by rubbing them with lemon juice.

CLEANING PURPLE MIMEOGRAPH INK FROM HANDS

Hairspray will remove purple mimeograph ink from your hands in a flash. Spray on, wipe off.

HEAVY-DUTY HAND CLEANER

Soda is a heavy-duty hand cleaner because it softens grime. Wet your hands and rub with dry baking soda.

FACE POWDER

Baby powder makes an excellent face powder.

PERSONAL GROOMING

BUFFING NAILS
An effective way to buff nails is to rub them vigorously across a chenille bedspread.

LIP GLOSS
For a non-greasy and inexpensive lip gloss, rub a dash of petroleum jelly over your lipstick. To condition dry lips, rub petroleum jelly over them after washing your face.

BLUSHER TIPS
1. For a cream blusher, color-coordinated with your lipstick, mix baby oil with your lipstick and apply over base make-up.
2. Rub a small amount of petroleum jelly on your cheeks before applying powder blusher to make it last longer.

TEETH WHITENER
Teeth will be whiter and brighter if polished with a little soda after the usual brushing.

MOUTHWASH
A healing mouthwash for inflamed gums can be made with soda, salt, and iodine. To 1 pint of water, add 1 teaspoon of salt, 1 teaspoon of soda, and ½ teaspoon of iodine. Used regularly, this will promote healthy gums.

REFRESHING COSMETICS
Cosmetics stored in the refrigerator are especially refreshing. This is particularly nice when vacationing at the beach.

CLEANING COMBS AND HAIRBRUSHES
Soak combs and brushes in household ammonia and water to get them squeaky clean. Dry brushes by placing the bristles down on a towel.

PERSONAL GROOMING

CONDITIONERS
FOR THE FACE
1. Mayonnaise is a soothing cream for skin that has been overexposed to sun, wind, or cold.
2. Baby lotion can be used as a face and body conditioner. Apply after bathing to slightly damp skin.
3. Avocados are good for your skin. Mash the pulp until it becomes a lumpless cream. (Add water if necessary.) Smooth this onto your face. Leave on 30 minutes, then rinse off.
4. Baby oil is an excellent moisturizer. After washing your face, pat on oil before applying make-up.
5. Fresh cream will make the skin soft and velvety. This should follow a masque treatment which tends to dry the skin.
6. Olive oil, corn oil, and solid shortening are excellent skin conditioners. Use as night cream or pat a thin coat of the oils on under make-up.

FOR THE BODY
1. A tablespoon of baby oil blended with ¼ cup of milk added to bath water will leave your skin feeling soft and smooth.
2. Rub the inside of an avocado peeling over elbows, feet, hands, and other dry spots. Leave this on a few minutes before showering. After this treatment your skin will feel smooth and soft.
3. A cupful of soda added to bath water softens skin and is very relaxing. Since soda will soften the water, this is especially nice if you live in an area where the water is hard.

FOR THE HAIR
1. For dry, brittle hair, use mayonnaise once a week as a conditioner. Apply to wet or dry hair, leave on for 30 minutes, then shampoo out.
2. In order to give your hair more body, treat it with the pulp of an avocado. Mash the avocado and massage it into your freshly-washed hair. Rub in and leave for 30 minutes before rinsing.
3. Give luster and shine to your hair by adding a few drops of baby lotion to the final rinse when shampooing.

PERSONAL GROOMING ════

FACIAL MASQUES

Three facial masques for tightening pores and toning the skin are:

1. Egg white masque: Slightly beat one egg white, pat on face and let dry. Add another layer and lie down for 30 minutes with the head lower than the body. Rinse with cool water.
2. Honey masque: Moisten face with water and apply room-temperature honey. This works even better if mixed with powdered milk. Leave awhile and then rinse off.
3. Soda and water masque: Make a paste of 2 tablespoons of soda and 3 tablespoons of water. Pat this mixture on your face and leave it for 10 minutes after it dries. Rinse off with cool water. This is especially good for removing blackheads.

DEODORANT

Soda can be used as a deodorant in an emergency. Pat on dry.

Reduce foot odor by dusting feet with soda or by sprinkling soda in your shoes.

MAKE-UP REMOVER CLOTHS

Men's old handkerchiefs make ideal make-up remover cloths for sensitive skin. Wash the handkerchiefs with your regular wash and do not worry about stains.

ITCH RELIEVER

Baking soda is a pain reliever for chicken pox or itching skin. First, soak in a tub of cool water to which has been added a cup of soda. After the bath, pat dry and sprinkle your skin with more soda. This is very effective.

SUNBURN TREATMENT

1. For a soothing sunburn treatment, mix 1 tablespoon of soda in a quart of cool water.
2. After being in the sun too long, splash vinegar on your sunburn to prevent peeling.

════PERSONAL GROOMING

MAKE-UP REMOVER

Baby oil is a gentle make-up
remover. Pat it on with your
fingertips, leave for 10 minutes,
remove with cotton balls.

ASTRINGENTS

1. Strong, effective astringents for oily skin are lemon juice or vinegar. Use several nights a week.
2. Mild astringents used to tighten the skin are grapes, strawberries, or cucumbers. Wash, slice, and rub over the face. Grapefruit juice is another mild astringent. Use about 3 times a week.

EYELASH CONDITIONERS

Rub lashes with petroleum jelly, baby oil, or baby lotion to condition them or for added shine instead of mascara.

CONTACT LENS TIPS

1. When inserting and removing lens, work over a smooth, flat surface which has a brightly colored linen towel over it. If dropped, the lens can be readily seen on the towel, and there will not be any lint from the linen.
2. Do not use hairspray after inserting lens; the spray can cause a difficult-to-remove film on the lens.

AVOIDING EYE INFECTIONS

Eye infections can be avoided by replacing old tubes of mascara every six months and keeping hands and applicators clean when applying make-up.

MOISTURIZING YOUR FACE

A plant mister filled with water is an easy way to moisturize your face before applying make-up and to eliminate the "made-up" look afterwards. Spray a light mist only.

PERSONAL GROOMING

RED SWOLLEN EYES
Red swollen eyes can be effectively treated in a short time by placing cold, wet tea bags on the lids and underneath the eyes for ten or fifteen minutes.

REMEDY FOR TIRED EYES
Soothe tired eyes by placing cucumber slices, slices of raw potatoes, or wet, cold teabags on the closed lids while resting.

HAIR RINSES
1. For blonde highlights: Rinse hair with ¼ cup of lemon juice mixed with ¾ cup of water.
2. For red highlights: Substitute vinegar for lemon juice and rinse hair with ¼ cup of vinegar mixed with ¾ cup of water.
3. To rid hair of every trace of hair spray, rinse with a teaspoon of soda added to a cup of water. Hair will feel soft and have an extra shine.

BURNING FEET
1. For a quick rest and pick-up for tired, burning feet, soak them in a pan of cool water with ¼ cup of soda.
2. After a hard day of standing or walking, try this. After your bath, rub your feet with baby oil, then pat on baby powder. This is very soothing.
3. Soak feet in a pan of warm water and 1 or 2 tablespoons of baby oil. This also softens calluses.

MINOR BURNS
1. Keep an aloe plant growing in your kitchen. When you get a minor burn, snip an aloe spike off and apply the cut end to the burn.
2. Another soothing remedy is to apply ice cubes to spot until the pain subsides.

Potpourri

POTPOURRI

IN THE BACKYARD
BUGS AND BITES
CAR CARE
CHILDREN'S CORNER
ETC., ETC., ETC.
FEATHERS, FINS, AND FUR
"BROWN THUMB" GARDENING TIPS
HINTS FOR HOLIDAYS
PENNY PINCHING

IN THE BACKYARD

GRILLS

COOKING ON THE GRILL:

Spray or rub your barbeque grill
with vegetable oil to prevent foods
from sticking to the grill.

REGULATING TEMPERATURE
WHEN CHARCOAL GRILLING:

Keep a plant mister filled with water by your charcoal
grill. When the fire gets too hot, or flames too high, mist
the coals with water.

MAKING CHARCOAL GRILLS LAST LONGER:

Keep charcoal grills from wearing out quickly by
putting a layer of sand on the bottom of the grill or by
lining the bottom of the grill with heavy-duty foil.

REFURBISHING OUTDOOR FURNITURE

OUTDOOR METAL FURNITURE:

Before applying a coat of paint to your metal furniture,
make sure it is free of rust and dirt.

Remove rust spots by scrubbing with a wire brush or
with coarse steel wool dipped in kerosene. After the rust
is removed, clean the entire piece with mineral spirits.
When the furniture is completely dry, paint with a
brush or spray paint.

REDWOOD FURNITURE:

Outdoor redwood furniture can be renewed and
preserved by "painting" it once a year with vegetable
oil. After 24 hours, rub off any excess oil.

CLEANING BRICK AND WOOD

BRICK TERRACES, FIREPLACES, PORCHES:

Clean the brick with muriatic acid. Scrub on with a stiff
brush and rinse with water. After the brick is
completely dry, apply a thin coat of sealer for a
beautiful finish.

CAUTION: When using muriatic acid, wear rubber
gloves and avoid getting on your skin or clothes. If you
are working indoors, make sure the room is ventilated.

POTPOURRI

MILDEWED WOOD:
Clean mildewed wooden decks or wood siding by scrubbing with this solution.

Mix:
  2 gallons of water
  2 cups of chlorine bleach
  1 cup of powdered detergent
  1 cup of powdered dishwashing detergent

Scrub wood with a stiff brush and rinse well.

CAUTION: To prevent damage to shrubs or grass, wet surrounding areas thoroughly *before* cleaning the wood as well as rinsing the greenery of all cleaning solution afterwards.

BUGS AND BITES

REDBUGS
PREVENTING REDBUG BITES:
Rub powdered sulphur around your waist, ankles, or any spot where clothing might fit tightly before going for a walk or picnic in the woods to prevent redbug bites. Sulphur can be bought at drugstores.

ALLEVIATING ITCHING FROM REDBUG BITES:
After walking or picnicking in the woods, try these remedies to alleviate itching from redbug bites:
1. Add ¼ cup of chlorine bleach to your bath water.
2. Scrub your body with yellow laundry soap while bathing.
3. If bites continue to bother you, paint spots with fingernail polish.

STINGS
BEE STINGS:
1. To relieve the pain and swelling from insect bites, apply a paste of soda and household ammonia to the sting. This works in a very short time.
2. Wet the tobacco from a cigarette and apply to the bite. This is especially helpful if on a picnic or away from home.
3. Another remedy for easing the pain is to wet the spot and sprinkle with meat tenderizer.

BUGS
BUG CONTROL:

One chemical is effective for many different kinds of household bugs. Liquid insecticides containing malathion help control:

ants	crickets
bedbugs	fleas
carpet beetles	weevils
clothes moths	scorpions
roaches	ticks

Spray the insecticide where you have seen these pests. Take care to cover dishes, glasses, silverware, and food before spraying.

CAR CARE

GENERAL HINTS
CORRODED CAR BATTERIES:

If your battery is corroded, pour a carbonated drink over it. This dissolves the corrosion.

BUGS ON CAR GRILL OR WINDSHIELD:

Remove bugs from the car grill or windshield by scrubbing with a nylon net ball and a mild liquid detergent and water. The net gives a little abrasion without scratching the car.

SQUEAKY CAR DOORS:

Stop the car door from squeaking by rubbing petroleum jelly on the hinges.

CAR STUCK IN SAND, MUD, OR SNOW:

1. To get your car unstuck, let a little air out of the tires and drive out.
2. Place boards, pieces of cardboard, or any flat surface in front of the tires and drive out.
3. Cars stuck in the snow can be driven out if you sprinkle cat litter on the snow all around the tires. Be prepared by keeping 1 or 2 bags (25 pounds) of litter in the car.

POTPOURRI

WASHING YOUR CAR
GENERAL HINTS:
1. Wash your car frequently with cold water and a mild detergent. Rinse thoroughly.
2. Don't wash your car with hot water.
3. Don't wash your car in the direct rays of the sun.
4. Don't wash your car while the car body is hot.

VINYL TOPS OR TRIM:
1. Wash often with mild soap suds and a brush with soft bristles. Make sure you rinse well to remove all traces of soap.
2. Don't use brushes with hard bristles or abrasive cleansers on vinyl tops or vinyl trim.

WINDOWS AND WINDSHIELDS:
1. Wash with clear water, mild liquid household cleaner, or a carbonated drink.
2. Don't wipe windows or windshield with a dry paper or cloth.

CHROME, CHROME-PLATED,
ALUMINUM TRIM:
1. Wash with water frequently and keep chrome and aluminum waxed and polished for protection.
2. Don't use heavy duty steel wool, abrasives, or strong detergents on chrome-plated or aluminum parts.
3. Don't use chrome polish on aluminum trim.

WHITE SIDEWALLS:
Scrub with soap, water, and a stiff brush, or steel wool and a cleanser.

UPHOLSTERY:
Vacuum upholstery regularly and clean with a sponge dipped in the suds from mild detergent and water. Do not saturate the upholstery. Immediately after cleaning, dry by rubbing vigorously with a terry cloth towel.

LEATHER TRIM:
Wash with a mild soap and damp cloth. Then rinse with a cloth dampened with clear water. Dry.

CHILDREN'S CORNER

GENERAL HINTS

CHEWING GUM IN HAIR:

Remove chewing gum from hair by rubbing the area with peanut butter, mayonnaise, or oil.

SHOPPING WITH CHILDREN:

Have children hold their hands together behind their backs when you must take them in a store. Shopkeepers really appreciate this, and the children like the game.

CHILDREN'S SQUABBLES:

Squabbles will become fewer if an egg-timer or an oven-timer is used to limit length of "turns" for playing with a toy or game. They can also be used for length of "time-out" punishments.

EMERGENCY TELEPHONE NUMBERS:

Children should be taught to dial *emergency telephone numbers* and to be able to give their first and last names and address clearly. Ask them to practice once a month.

PLAYTIME

CHALK DRAWINGS:

Prevent smudges and having the chalk rub off onto your clothes by using hairspray as a fixative. Simply spray the finished drawing lightly and allow to dry.

PAINT CONTAINERS:

Muffin pans make excellent containers for children's fingerpaints or temperas.

PAINT SHIRTS:

1. One of Daddy's old dress shirts can be used for a paint shirt. Put it on backwards, button the top button only, and roll up the sleeves to the desired length.
2. Even better for a paint shirt is one of Daddy's old tee shirts. It can be slipped on easier, and there are no buttons to be buttoned. Let the young artist "paint" designs on it with permanent magic markers.

81

POTPOURRI

TEMPERA PAINT TIP:

Add a teaspoonful or capful of liquid detergent to each cup of paint. This makes tempera stains easier to wash out.

PLAY DOUGH RECIPE:

1 cup flour	2 tablespoons oil
1 cup water	2 teaspoons cream of tartar
½ cup salt	

Cook 3 minutes.

Before cooking, add a few drops of food coloring, if desired, to the water.

This makes a good dough for Christmas tree ornaments.

Roll the dough out on wax paper, using cookie cutters to make the ornaments. Be sure to punch a small hole near the top for a string or ornament hanger before the dough hardens.

Bake in a slow oven for about 40 minutes.

The ornaments can be painted with tempera and glazed if the dough has not been colored.

To glaze the ornaments, mix 1 cup of white liquid glue with 1 cup of water. When tempera is completely dry, apply glaze with a brush.

CHILDREN'S PARTIES GENERAL HINTS:

1. Serve ice cream in a small terra cotta or plastic flowerpot. Attach a plastic flower to a brightly colored plastic spoon and stick it in the ice cream.
2. Cute candle holders for birthday cakes or cupcakes are lifesaver candies.
3. A colorful, tasty treat to serve at children's parties is peppermint lemonade. To make this treat, cut the top off a lemon and insert a peppermint stick which acts as a straw. When the lemon juice is sucked through the peppermint stick, it makes a delicious peppermint lemonade. Children love it!

SAFETY FOR CHILDREN
GENERAL HINTS:
1. Place decals or colored tape on glass sliding doors at the child's eye level as well as the adult's eye level.
2. Tape light cords tightly around table legs to prevent children from pulling the lamps onto the floor. Transparent tape will not mar the furniture.
3. Prevent fingers from being mashed by a piano lid by placing corks on either end of the keyboard. If the lid drops, the cork gets the blow.
4. Tie jingle bells on all doors (outside doors as well as cabinet doors) that you don't want your child to open. When you hear the ring you will know exactly where he is and what he is doing.

EMERGENCY PROCEDURES:
Children should be taught emergency procedures in case of a fire or tornado and have monthly practice drills at home. They should be trained to use the established plans rather than going to the parents' room. This could save their lives.

CHILD SAFETY ON OUTINGS:
When you are on family picnics or camping trips, give each child a whistle to blow in case of an emergency. An emergency could cover everything from a bee sting to spotting a snake or getting separated from the group. In this way, parents can relax, yet still be on duty.

HALLOWEEN SAFETY:
1. Costumes should have some white or light areas so that they can be seen readily.
2. For added protection, reflective tape should be sewn on the hem, sleeves, and top of the costume.
3. Costumes should also be flame-proof.
4. Masks should offer children adequate visibility.
5. Adults should accompany the children on their route.
6. Children should carry a flashlight rather than a candle.
7. Apples, candy, or other treats should be examined by an adult before eaten.
8. It is safest to trick-or-treat at the homes of friends.

POTPOURRI

CLOTHING
SOCK BASKET:
When all of the children wear the same size socks, store clean socks in a big basket centrally located. This saves sorting time and helps develop the child's independence since he can get his own socks each morning.

CLOTHES IDENTIFICATION:
Non-reading children can identify their jackets, caps, or mittens readily if a unique button (from Dad's old army jacket perhaps) is attached to the garment.

EDUCATIONAL
GROWING THINGS:
1. Dried lima beans make a good, quick demonstration of plant life. Soak beans overnight in water, then plant in soil using a clear plastic flowerpot or glass for a container. Push the seeds so they are visible through the side of the container. Water and place in the sunlight. Growth should begin in twenty-four hours.
2. Tops of carrots placed in a small amount of water will soon provide lacy, green foliage. The carrot section should be about one inch thick.

CONTAINERS FOR COLLECTIONS:
Egg cartons make excellent containers for children's rock, shell, or bug collections.

ETC., ETC., ETC.
FLOWERS AND FRAGRANCES
DRIED FLOWERS:
Wildflowers, hydrangeas, or other flowers from woody plants can be dried and preserved by cutting and hanging upside down for a few weeks. For a little added protection, spray with hairspray before arranging.

KEEPING FLOWERS FRESH:
Keep cut flowers fresh longer by placing in a quart of warm water to which has been added 2 tablespoons of vinegar and 3 tablespoons of sugar.

TULIP TIPS:

When arranging tulips, always remove tough white fibrous portion from the lower stems. Do this with a long diagonal cut so the stems can absorb as much water as possible. Also, remove unnecessary foliage to prolong the life of the blooms. Gently peel all but the top two leaves from the tulip stem. Use the extra leaves separately to fill out your arrangement. To keep the tulip flower from closing, drop one or two drops of melted wax into the center of each bloom.

PORCELAINIZED FLOWERS:

Mix in a large can:
  1 pint of high gloss white enamel
  1 pint of varnish
  ½ pint of turpentine

Dust, wash, and air dry plastic flowers. Then dip each flower into the glaze individually. Shake off excess and stand flowers in a soft drink bottle to dry. After flowers have dried, they are ready for arranging.

ROOM FRESHENER:

Make your rooms smell delightful by placing an opened container of room freshener in front of the air-conditioning or heating unit filter. Replace with a new one each time you replace the filter.

POMANDERS:

Pomanders can be made out of apples, oranges, lemons, whole cloves, and cinnamon. Push the cloves close together in the fruit, and do not leave any skin area unfilled. Roll the fruit in cinnamon after the cloves are in place. Group the pomanders in a bowl for a room freshener, place them in a drawer, or hang them by a ribbon in your closet.

CONVERSION OF METRIC MEASUREMENTS ON MATTRESSES

Use this guide for buying mattresses which are labeled in metric measurements only.

TWIN	38" x 75"	or 0.97 x 1.92 meters
FULL	53" x 75"	or 1.36 x 1.92 meters
QUEEN	60" x 80"	or 1.54 x 2.05 meters
KING	76" x 80"	or 1.95 x 2.05 meters

POTPOURRI

REMOVING CAPS FROM TUBES
Remove stubborn caps from tubes of glue or paint easily by holding a lighted match under the cap for a few seconds.

BAITING MOUSETRAPS
Bait mousetraps with peanut butter rather than cheese. The peanut butter can't slip out of the trap, and your chances of catching the mouse are greater.

PAINTING WIRE FENCES
Paint wire fences the easy way by using a sponge instead of a brush. Put the paint in a flat aluminum pan you can dip the sponge in without difficulty.

PICKING UP TINY GLASS SLIVERS
Tiny slivers of broken glass can be picked up easily by rubbing a wet paper towel or paper napkin over the fragments.

TAKING THE ITCH OUT OF POISON IVY RASHES
If you have poison ivy, try these for relief of symptoms:
1. Pat rash with a weak solution of chlorine bleach and water.
2. Soak in a tub of lukewarm water mixed with a cup of baking soda.

POSTAGE STAMPS STUCK TOGETHER
If your postage stamps have become stuck together, place them between two pieces of brown paper and iron them with a hot iron. While they are hot they can be separated.

SHELF OR DRAWER LINING
Freezer paper makes inexpensive shelf or drawer lining. Place shiny side out.

PRESERVING NEWSPAPER CLIPPINGS, RECIPES, OR CHILDREN'S DRAWINGS

Newspaper clippings or recipes can be easily preserved by covering them with clear contact paper. To make them stiffer, place the clipping on a piece of cardboard before wrapping with the contact paper.

SNOW SAFETY

Snow-covered driveways and walks can be spread with cat litter to make them safe for walking.

FEATHERS, FINS, AND FUR

BIRDS

MAKING BIRDFEEDERS SQUIRREL-PROOF:

Apply a heavy coat of petroleum jelly to the birdfeeder pole. The squirrels cannot climb it, and it won't hurt them. When the jelly wears off, reapply it.

BIRD FOOD:

Birds eat a variety of foods in addition to wild berries and commercially prepared foods. They also like:
1. Popped popcorn.
2. Peanut butter and seeds formed into little balls.
3. Suet mixed with seeds.
4. Seeds from watermelons, squash, sunflowers, and pumpkins.

If you start feeding the birds during the winter months, keep it up the entire winter. Once they become dependent upon your help, it is difficult for them to locate food on their own.

BLUEBIRD HOUSE:

A ½ gallon juice can painted black makes a good bluebird house. After removing one end, spray the can black, let dry, and attach it to a post or tree 4 feet from the ground near some bushes.

POTPOURRI

DOGS AND CATS
CAT'S FUR BALLS:
To help your cat get rid of unwanted fur balls, place a dab of petroleum jelly on his nose which when licked turns into mineral oil.

DOGHOUSES:
1. Keep doghouses clean and smelling fresh by washing with a mixture of water and ½ cup of pine oil.
2. Place pine straw or cedar chips in the doghouse for comfortable bedding and to keep down odors.

FLEAS ON PETS:
Powder your pets with a dust containing 4% malathion to get rid of fleas. This dust is safe for cats and dogs and can be bought at hardware stores or garden supply stores.

GLOSSY COATS FOR YOUR PETS:
Your pets' coats will shine if you add one of the following to their diets each day:
1. Two or 3 tablespoons of melted animal fat to your pet's food. Vegetable fat is not effective.
2. Two or 3 tablespoons of debittered brewers' yeast.
3. Raw egg.

CRYING PUPPIES:
1. Put a ticking clock in your new puppy's box to keep him from crying.
2. Put a pair of socks that have been worn by the owner in the puppy's bed. The scent of the new master gives him security.

SKUNK SHOWER:
If your dog is showered by a skunk, wash him in tomato juice to remove the odor.

DOGGY ODORS:
Place a small uncovered bowl of vinegar in a sick room or in the room where your pet sleeps. The vinegar will absorb the unpleasant odors.

ODORLESS KITTY SANDBOX:

To absorb the odors in your cat's sandbox, fill the box with either one of the following combinations:
1. Borax and kitty litter — 1 part borax to 6 parts litter.
2. Baking soda and kitty litter — 1 cup of soda added to the litter.

FISH

FISH BOWL CLEANING:

Do not use soap on a fish bowl. This will kill the fish.

"BROWN THUMB" GARDENING TIPS

PLANTS, FLOWERS AND FERNS

ALOE PLANTS:

Aloe plants thrive on neglect. Place in a sunny window and water infrequently.

CLEANING HOUSEPLANTS:

1. Remove dust with a cloth or feather duster.
2. Give a gloss to the leaves by rubbing with one of the following:

   mayonnaise   baby oil
   olive oil   glycerine
   solution of half milk, half water

NOTE: The glycerine and the milk solution are preferred since they will not attract dust.

DISEASED PLANTS:

If your houseplants have mealy bugs or scale on them, spray plants with a mixture of one-half rubbing alcohol and one-half water. Stubborn areas can be further treated by rubbing with a cotton swab dipped in the mixture and then spraying again.

FERNS:

Ferns like being "watered" with weak tea or soapy water.

POTPOURRI

GERANIUMS:

Geraniums like at least a half day of sunshine, a container which will allow the water to drain out, and a dry soil. When fertilizing, always wet the soil first before adding the fertilizer. This will keep it from burning the plants.

CHANGING THE COLOR OF HYDRANGEAS:

You can change the color of your hydrangeas to suit your color scheme by using these tricks:
1. Blue hydrangeas will be the result if you keep rusty nails in the dirt close to the plant.
2. Pink hydrangeas will be the result if you sprinkle lime around the plant.

PINEAPPLE PLANTS:

Pineapple plants can be grown easily by planting the top of a fresh pineapple in a mixture of potting soil and sand. Place it in the sun, water occasionally, and be patient. If you wait long enough it will grow a small pineapple.

PHILODENDRON AND SNAKE PLANTS:

Philodendron and snake plants (Sansevieria) can be grown successfully and effortlessly in strong or dim light, water or soil, frequent or infrequent waterings. You can't fail with these two.

WATERING PLANTS WHILE ON VACATION:

Plants can be watered while you are on vacation by using a heavy cord and a glass of water. Put the glass of water next to your plant, bury one end of the cord in the soil, put the other end in the water. The water will travel from glass to plant via the cord.

VIOLETS:

It is no problem to have lovely violets blooming year round in your home. Make sure the container your violet is in has a hole in the bottom. Place the pot in a saucer and fill the saucer once a week with a water-fertilizer solution. Keep the violet in a sunny window.

Violets can even be grown in water. If your plants refuse to do well in soil, place the plant in water and watch it bloom.

SEEDS, VINES, AND BULBS
AVOCADO SEEDS:

Avocado seeds grow into attractive houseplants with little effort from the gardener. Stick toothpicks around the middle of the seed, rest the picks on the rim of a glass or jar with the large end in the water and the small end above the container. In a short time roots will appear. After several leaves have sprouted and a good root system has developed, transplant to a potting medium and water once a week.

LEMON, ORANGE, AND GRAPEFRUIT SEEDS:

Plants can be grown from seeds from oranges, lemons, or grapefruits. Plant the seeds in potting soil and keep them in a sunny window or plant them outdoors if you live in the South.

SWEET POTATO VINE:

Grow a lush vine by submerging half of a sweet potato in a glass of water. Roots and leaves will soon appear. This will provide you with a beautiful plant for months.

STORING BULBS:

Bulbs can be stored in the mesh bags fruit comes in or in snagged pantyhose. Hang the bulbs up so that the air can circulate around them.

GARDEN PESTS
PREVENTING NEMATODES ON TOMATOES:

Keep nematodes from attacking your tomatoes by planting marigolds around each tomato plant.

PROTECTING YOUR GARDEN FROM PESTS:

1. Sprinkle red pepper on the new green shoots of your prize bulbs to keep the rabbits from eating them.
2. Sprinkle moth balls or moth crystals over your lawn and around shrubs to keep dogs, cats, squirrels, and snakes away.

POTPOURRI

HANDS AND KNEES
HAND CARE WHILE GARDENING:
Your hands need not suffer while you are gardening if you do these tricks:

1. Scrape your fingernails over a bar of soap before you begin your outside work. This makes it much easier to clean your nails later even if you wear gloves.
2. Put lotion on your hands before putting on your gardening gloves. Your hands will be better protected, plus getting a treatment.

GARDEN KNEELING PAD:
Use a child's plastic kindergarten mat as a kneeling pad when gardening. This is much more comfortable, and the mat is not damaged by moist or wet soil.

TOOLS
PREVENTING RUSTY TOOLS:
Fill a bucket or any similar container with sand, saturate with oil, and stick shovels, hoes, or other garden tools in the sand. This prevents the tools from rusting. Any oil can be used.

REMOVING RUST FROM IRON TOOLS:
Remove rust from iron tools by scrubbing the rust spots with steel wool dipped in kerosene.

HINTS FOR HOLIDAYS

CHRISTMAS
SNOW FOR THE CHRISTMAS TREE:
Snow for your Christmas tree can be made from a thick solution of powdered soap flakes and water. Beat at high speed with an electric mixer until the mixture is stiff. Spoon on the tree branches and limbs. This makes an unbelievably beautiful tree.

GIFT TAGS:
The beautiful pictures on old Christmas cards can be clipped off and used as lovely gift tags.

LONGLASTING CHRISTMAS TREES:

1. When buying Christmas trees, check for freshness by rubbing your finger across the cut side of the base. If the stump is gooey with sap, it is a fresh tree.
2. Douglas fir, spruce, and Scotch pine hold their needles better than other varieties.
3. To keep the needles greener longer, cut an extra inch or two from the bottom of the tree and stand the tree in a bucket of cold water to which one cup of sugar, molasses, syrup, or honey has been added. Let the tree soak for 2 or 3 days prior to decorating.

UNIQUE WRAPPING PAPER:

Use newspapers for wrapping gifts. Big packages wrapped in this manner and tied with red ribbon are especially eye-catching. Use wide-tipped felt pens for writing the "to" and "from" names. Children's gifts could be wrapped in the Sunday comics.

HARVEST DOOR DECORATIONS:

Use broomstraw, so disliked by modern farmers, to make charming and useful brooms. Collect the straw any time during the winter after it has shed its blooms. Strip off the blades up to about 15 inches from the bottom for the handle. Give it a good shaking to get rid of any remaining blooms. Now take a bundle of straw about 2 inches in diameter, spread the ends you plan to use for a handle on waxed paper and give them a good coat of waterproof glue or plastic cement. Make sure that the glue touches each straw at some point. Wind a brightly-colored cord tightly around the straw about 15 inches from the end, a dozen or so times, to make a band ¾ inches wide. Then move 3 or 4 inches down the handle and make another. Repeat the bands until you reach the end. Fasten the cord by weaving back and forth between ends of the straw. When thoroughly dry, shellac the handle, and the broom is ready for use as a harvest door decoration.

CHRISTMAS WREATHS:

Lovely Christmas wreaths can be made from grape or wisteria vines by twisting vines together the size of the wreath you want. Fasten with florist wire or twist ties. Add a colorful bow, and you will have an eye-catching door decoration.

POTPOURRI

PENNY PINCHING

BUDGETING

REDUCING AIR-CONDITIONER COSTS:

1. Keep the sun out by converting your house into a cocoon. Close draperies, shades, or shutters during the day, especially on the east and west sides, to keep the sun out. At night, open the draperies to let the cooler air in.
2. Use fans along with the air-conditioner to keep air circulating.
3. Plant trees and vines to act as shades outside the house. Be sure to space the tree far enough from the house to provide growing room.

TRIM THE BUDGET:

1. Save 10 - 20% by using store brands. Save even more by using generic brands.
2. Save up to 15% by comparison shopping of goods and services.
3. Save 15% or more on day-old bakery products.
4. Save 6 - 30% by paying cash instead of using credit.
5. Save up to 15% by buying the promotional sales items.
6. Save up to 18% on cosmetics by using less well-known products or shopping special sales of name brands.
7. Save 10 - 18% on your new car by not buying one with extra features.

ENERGY TIPS:

1. It is more efficient to cool or freeze food than to cool empty space; therefore, when buying a refrigerator or freezer, don't overestimate your needs.
2. Window shades form a better barrier against heat flow than draperies. In cold weather, three to four times more heat escapes through window glass than through the sash area around the window. Snug-fitting window shades within the frame can block heat loss by 24-31%.
3. At night lower the shades and let up during the day during winter. In summer, heat build up can be reduced as much as one-half by keeping shades lowered during the hot, sunny hours.

ENERGY TIPS (cont.)

4. Baking potatoes in a toaster oven uses about half the energy required by a full-sized electric oven.

GAMES TO HELP YOU SAVE MONEY:

The Cookie Jar Game — Every night empty all your change into the cookie jar. Every other month roll the coins in proper wrappers and add the money to a special account.

The Special Coin Game — Let every member of the family save dimes, nickels, or quarters for a given period of time, then do something special with the money. (Dinner out, a movie, family game.)

The Windfall Game — Whenever you receive any unexpected money such as refunds, birthday money, or money from a garage sale, put it into a savings account.

The Swap-A-Habit Game — Choose a habit you would like to conquer. Instead of spending money on your habit, deposit that exact amount and watch your savings grow.

The Self-Service Game — Reduce the amount of money you spend on services and begin to do them yourself. Pay yourself what you formerly paid someone else to do.

The Don't See It, Don't Spend It Game — Sign up for a payroll deduction plan with your job.

The Income Tax Refund Game — Claim fewer exemptions for dependents on the W-4 employee withholding tax form at work. Eventually you will be able to bank the refund.

LIGHTING TIPS:

1. One watt of fluorescent lighting gives 4 times as much light as a watt of incandescent, and the fluorescent bulb lasts 15 to 25 times longer.
2. Dust on bulbs can reduce the light by 50%, so keep bulbs dusted.
3. "Long-life" bulbs give less light than standard bulbs of the same wattage. Use them only in hard-to-get-to locations where a high level of light is not important.

POTPOURRI ══════════════

FREEZER EFFICIENCY TIPS:

1. Be sure to allow space for air circulation around the freezer. If the freezer is placed in a closet or small storage room, it may be necessary to leave the storage room door open slightly. Without adequate ventilation the freezer will have to work overtime to do its job, using more energy and causing unnecessary wear on the motor.
2. A freezer operates most efficiently when it is more than ¾ full. Jamming in too much food restricts the air circulation necessary for cooling, and running a nearly empty freezer wastes the cold air.
3. For best results a freezer should maintain a temperature of zero degrees Fahrenheit.
4. In order to keep foods cold enough, do not allow the frost level to build up on a manual defrost freezer more than ¼ inch.

POWER FAILURE TIP FOR FREEZERS:

1. With the power off, a loaded freezer should keep the foods frozen for two days if the door stays shut.
2. If the foods should thaw, never refreeze vegetables, casseroles, melted ice cream, meat, soups, seafoods, or fruit juice concentrates.
3. Thawed breads and unfrosted cakes can be refrozen.

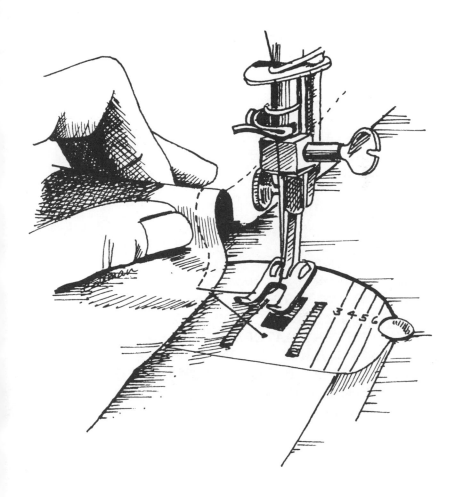

Sewing

SEWING

SEWING ON BUTTONS

Buttons will stay on longer if sewn on with:

1. 4 strands of thread
2. dental floss

BUTTON BOXES

1. An empty ½ pint or pint jar with lid makes a good bottom container and doesn't take up too much space in your sewing basket. With a clear jar you can find the buttons you need without emptying the contents.
2. Plastic zipper boxes make ideal storage for buttons that are cut from old garments.

BUTTONHOLES

For perfect-sized buttonholes, make sample buttonholes of various sizes on a strip of cloth and write the sizes under each. Use this as a buttonhole gauge.

ZIPPERS

1. Metal zippers should be used on blue jeans or jackets.
2. Nylon zippers should be used on delicate fabrics.
3. Balky zippers will zip more smoothly if rubbed with paraffin or a candle.

REMOVING OLD HEMLINE CREASES

After lowering the hem on a wool garment, sponge the old hemline with vinegar before pressing. This removes the telltale crease.

DESIGNS FOR EMBROIDERING AND STENCILING

Soap slivers can be used for drawing a design for embroidery, stenciling, or appliquéing if you are working on a washable material. Erasing errors in design is done quickly by dabbing with a soft sponge or cloth wrung out in water. When the design is completed, wash the garment to remove the pattern. The soap crayon can be whittled from a sliver of soap with a sharp knife.

SEWING

SEWING MACHINE CARE
1. Oil and delint your machine at least once a month if used regularly.
2. Oil by putting one drop of oil on each moving part.
3. Delint by brushing each part of the machine with a small paintbrush.
4. Use a lightweight oil; never a heavy oil.
5. Never oil, or try to oil, the motor of your sewing machine.
6. When not in use, keep your machine closed to prevent it from collecting dust.

BEFORE CALLING THE REPAIRMAN
Try:
1. A new needle
2. Oiling the machine
3. Delinting the machine

STUFFING DOLLS, PILLOWS, OR TOYS
Stuff dolls, pillows, or toys with old stockings or panty hose. This makes a soft, washable stuffing.

SEWING WITH SHEETS AND PILLOWCASES
When using sheets and pillowcases for curtains, tablecloths, or other household decorating, figure the yardage as follows:
1 twin size flat sheet — 5-1/4 yards
1 full size flat sheet — 6-1/2 yards
1 queen size flat sheet — 7-1/2 yards
1 king size flat sheet — 9-1/8 yards
1 standard size pillowcase — 1-1/8 yards
1 king size pillowcase — 1-3/8 yards

SEWING TABLECLOTHS AND CURTAINS
Brightly colored sheets make lovely tablecloths and curtains without ruining the budget.

MENDING POCKETS
When pockets are wearing thin, reinforce them with iron-on tape. This prevents holes from wearing in the pockets.

PREVENT KNOTTING OF THREAD
To prevent knotting of thread when hemming or basting, tie your knot in the thread before you cut it off the spool.

CUTTING VELVETEEN, VELVET, CORDUROY
Cut these three fabrics when the pile is all going in the same direction.

SEWING ON ...
PLAID
When matching plaids before sewing, pin the pieces together with needles rather than pins. Sewing machines glide easier over needles, and the plaids will stay in place better.

WOOL
Silk thread is the best type to use in sewing wool.

UNSHRUNK MATERIAL
Unbleached muslin or any unshrunk material should be washed, dried, and ironed before cutting and sewing.

SLIPPERY MATERIAL
Slippery material won't slide as you sew if you wrap a turkish towel around the leaf of your sewing machine.

PREVENTING OIL STAINS ON FABRICS WHEN MACHINE SEWING
After oiling your machine, stitch several rows on a paper towel or scrap cloth before stitching on garments or fabrics. The paper towel and scrap cloth will absorb any excess oil.

SEWING

MARKING HEMS
1. White chalk or a white nail pencil is excellent for marking hems.
2. Talcum powder can be used effectively in professional hem markers.
3. Slivers of soap can be used for marking hems on washable fabrics.

PINCUSHIONS
1. For sharp needles and pins fill pincushions with human hair or steel wool.
2. Corduroy, felt, and suede make good pincushion covers.
3. A 3 inch width of felt placed around the slender middle section of a sewing machine is an excellent pincushion for needles and pins.

PINS
The sharpest pins are ballpoint stainless steel. The sharper the pin, the less danger of picking the fabric.

DRAPERY WEIGHTS
Fishing sinkers make excellent weights for curtains and draperies. These weights can be bought in most sporting goods departments.

SHARPENING SCISSORS / SCISSORS NEEDED
1. Emergency sharpening can be done by cutting aluminum foil several times.
2. If possible, get your scissors sharpened professionally.
3. Cutting sandpaper to sharpen your scissors ruins them.
4. Do not try to sharpen your scissors with a file. This also ruins them.

Every homemaker needs three different pairs of scissors:
1. Small scissors for buttonholes and delicate work.
2. Medium-sized scissors for clipping seams and curves.
3. Scissors about 7 inches long for general cutting.

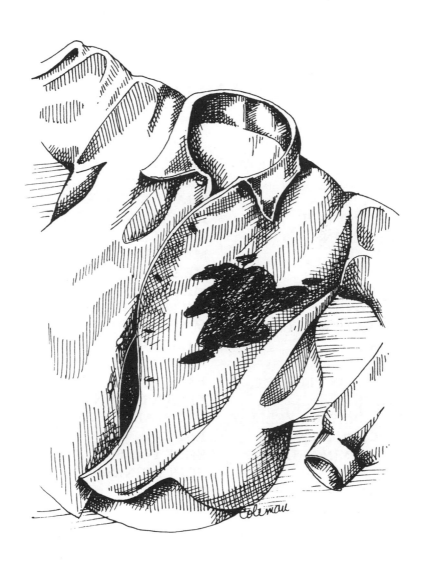

Spots and Stains

SPOTS AND STAINS

SPOTS AND STAINS

GENERAL HINTS FOR STAIN REMOVAL

1. Treat spots and soiled areas as quickly as possible to reduce the chance of having a permanent stain.
2. If possible, test the treatment first on a part of the fabric hidden from view, such as the hem or facing.
3. Soak mild or new spots 30 minutes before washing. Soak severe or old stains several hours. Be sure to use enough detergent or enzyme product to be effective in removing the soil.
4. Enzyme products are most effective in warm water. They are not effective when used with chlorine bleach.
5. Use an oxygen bleach rather than a chlorine bleach if the water in your area contains iron. Chlorine bleach used with water which contains iron will make rust discoloration worse.
6. Protein stains are set by hot water; therefore, soak these stains in cold water before washing in hot water.
7. Treat sugar stains with water and a mild detergent.
8. Treat grease stains with mineral spirits.
9. Treat combination stains (sugar and grease as in pies) with both sugar and grease removers.
10. For dry cleanable fabrics only, be sure to tell the cleaner the cause of the spot.

BROWN STAINS

Stains that have become set and turned brown cannot be completely removed, but bleaching with a chlorine bleach will lighten them somewhat.

TEA

WASHABLE FABRICS:

Soak at once in cold water with a detergent. When spot is removed, wash garment in hot water and a detergent.

NON-WASHABLE FABRICS:

Before taking to a professional dry cleaners, sponge the spot with cold water.

CARPET:

Blot immediately and scrub with a towel dampened with clear water.

SPOTS AND STAINS ══════════

SOFT DRINKS

WASHABLE FABRICS:

Soak in cold water with a small amount of mild liquid detergent and 1 tablespoon of white vinegar for 15 minutes. Rinse with clear water. If stain remains, sponge with rubbing alcohol and wash. If stain still remains, soak in 1 quart of warm water and 1 tablespoon of an enzyme pre-soak product for 30 minutes, then wash.

NON-WASHABLE FABRICS:

Before taking to a professional dry cleaners, sponge with a mild detergent and water.

CARPET:

First, scrub stain with a towel wrung out in cold water. After removing as much of the stain as possible with water only, scrub the spot with cold water and a mild detergent. Be sure to rinse thoroughly and remove all traces of the detergent.

EGG

WASHABLE FABRICS:

Soak in cold water with a detergent or enzyme pre-soak product. When stain is removed, wash garment in hot water and a detergent.

EGGNOG

FRESH SPILL AT A PARTY:

Use a spoon or knife to lift off the excess. With a napkin, blot up as much liquid as possible. Rub spot with a cloth dampened with clear water.

WASHABLE FABRICS:

As soon as possible, soak in cold water with an enzyme pre-soak product. When spot is removed wash garment in hot water and a detergent.

NON-WASHABLE FABRICS:

Before sending to a professional dry cleaners, sponge with water and a mild detergent.

WINE

AT A PARTY:

Sprinkle table salt on the stain to absorb it. When the salt dries, brush it off.

WASHABLE FABRICS:

Soak spot in cold water. When spot is removed, wash as usual.

NON-WASHABLE FABRICS:

Sponge with cool water before sending to a professional dry cleaners.

CARPET:

Blot the stain with paper towels, then sprinkle with salt. Leave the salt on overnight, then vacuum. If any stain remains, scrub vigorously with a terry cloth towel wrung out with cold water.

FRUIT AND FRUIT JUICES

WASHABLE FABRICS:

Soak in 1 quart of warm water with ¼ teaspoon of mild liquid detergent and 1 tablespoon of white vinegar for 15 minutes. Rinse with clear water. If stain remains, sponge with rubbing alcohol and wash. If stain still remains, soak in 1 quart of warm water and 1 tablespoon of an enzyme pre-soak product for 30 minutes; then wash.

NON-WASHABLE FABRICS:

Take immediately to a professional dry cleaners.

CAUTION: Do not use soap on fruit juice stains because that sets them.

MILK AND CREAM

WASHABLE FABRICS:

Pre-treat by soaking in cold water with a detergent or an enzyme product. When spot is removed, wash garment in hot water and a detergent.

SPOTS AND STAINS ═══════════

CHOCOLATE AND COCOA
WASHABLE FABRICS:
Prewash by soaking in warm water and a detergent. When stain is removed, wash garment in hot water, detergent, and a bleach.

NON-WASHABLE FABRICS:
Before having the garment professionally dry-cleaned, sponge with warm water and a mild detergent.

ICE CREAM
WASHABLE FABRICS:
Soak in cold water with a detergent or enzyme product before washing. When the spot is removed, wash in hot water with a detergent.

NON-WASHABLE FABRICS:
Before sending to a professional dry cleaners, sponge with a mild detergent and cold water.

MUSTARD
WASHABLE FABRICS:
Wash out the garment in cold water before rubbing the stain with heavy-duty, yellow laundry soap. Soak overnight in cold water with the soap. If stain still is visible, it may be necessary to bleach it if fabric permits.

NON-WASHABLE FABRICS:
Sponge with cold water before taking to a professional dry cleaners.

CARPET AND UPHOLSTERY:
After removing as much of the mustard as possible with a knife blade, scrub with one of the following:
1. Cold water
2. 1 teaspoon of a mild detergent to 1 cup water
3. ¼ cup of white vinegar to 1 cup water

COFFEE

WASHABLE FABRICS:

Rub garment or linens with a yellow, heavy-duty laundry soap, and soak in cold water overnight. Before washing, scrub stain thoroughly. If stain remains, continue to rub with the laundry soap and soak until removed. When there is no trace of the stain left, wash in hot water and detergent.

NON-WASHABLE FABRICS:

Sponge spot immediately with cold water before taking to a professional dry cleaners.

CARPET:

Scrub carpet immediately with a terry cloth towel wrung out in cold water.

MEAT JUICE (not gravy)

WASHABLE FABRICS:

Pre-treat by soaking in cold water and a non-chlorine bleach. When spot is completely removed, wash garment in hot water and a detergent.

NON-WASHABLE FABRICS:

Blot juice immediately and sponge with cold water. Sponge longer than you think is necessary to remove every trace. When garment dries, send it to a professional cleaners.

CARPET AND UPHOLSTERY:

Blot juice immediately and sponge with a terry cloth towel wrung out in cold water. Rub in a circular motion and rinse towel frequently. When spot is removed, rub with a dry towel. It is helpful to use a white towel when removing the spot.

BABY FORMULA

Soak in cold water with a detergent or enzyme soap product for 30 minutes or until spot is removed. When spot is removed, wash garment in hot water and a detergent.

SPOTS AND STAINS ══════════

CATSUP
WASHABLE FABRICS:
Prewash by soaking in cold water with a detergent. When spot is removed, wash garment in hot water and a detergent.
NON-WASHABLE FABRICS:
Before having the garment professionally cleaned, sponge with water and a mild detergent.

GRAVY, GREASE, OR OIL
WASHABLE FABRICS:
Pre-treat by rubbing liquid detergent or a liquid enzyme product directly on the spot. Allow to stand several hours; wash in hot water with a detergent.
NON-WASHABLE FABRICS:
Before taking to a professional dry cleaners, sponge the spot with mineral spirits.
CARPET:
Use this procedure for removing gravy, grease, or oil stains from carpets:
1. Blot the spill immediately with paper towels. Do not rub.
2. Sprinkle baking soda, cornmeal, or baby powder on grease spots. Leave on overnight and then vacuum.
3. Sponge the spot with mineral spirits. Rub with a circular motion, using a terry cloth towel.

BALL POINT PEN
First try removing the spot with one or all of these:
dry-cleaning fluid
rubbing alcohol
hairspray
WASHABLE FABRICS:
When spot is removed, wash garment as usual.
NON-WASHABLE FABRICS:
When spot is removed, take the garment to a professional cleaners.

CHEWING GUM

WASHABLE FABRICS:

Rub gum with an ice cube to chill and harden it for easier removal. Scrape off as much as possible with a knife before sponging with mineral spirits. Air dry, then wash as usual.

NON-WASHABLE FABRICS:

Rub gum with an ice cube to chill and harden it for easier removal. Scrape off as much as possible with a knife before sponging with mineral spirits. Air dry, then have professionally cleaned.

CARPET AND UPHOLSTERY:

Rub gum with an ice cube to chill and harden it for easier removal. Scrape off as much as possible with a knife before sponging with mineral spirits.

CRAYONS

WASHABLE FABRICS:

Pre-treat by rubbing liquid detergent or a paste made from powdered detergent and water directly onto the stain. Allow to stand overnight. Wash in hot water and a detergent.

NON-WASHABLE FABRICS:

Before sending to a professional dry cleaners, sponge the stain with mineral spirits.

MIMEOGRAPH INK

WASHABLE FABRICS:

Spray hairspray on spot and rub immediately with a cloth. Repeat until ink is removed. Wash garment as usual.

NON-WASHABLE FABRICS:

Spray hairspray on spot and rub immediately with a cloth. Be sure to rub gently on non-washable fabrics. Repeat if necessary before sending to a professional dry cleaners.

SPOTS AND STAINS ═══════

PAINT
WASHABLE FABRICS:
Tempera paint:

Pre-treat by soaking in cold water with a detergent. When spot is removed, wash garment in hot water and a detergent.

Oil-based paint:

Sponge or soak in turpentine for 30 minutes. Rinse out turpentine and air dry. After garment is completely dry, rub detergent into stain and soak in hot water for one hour. After stain is removed, wash as usual.

DRY-CLEANING FLUID
WASHABLE FABRICS:
A ring on permanent press fabrics caused by dry-cleaning fluid cannot be washed out. Clean the garment in a coin-operated dry cleaner or send to a professional dry cleaners.

FABRIC SOFTENER
WASHABLE FABRICS:
Rub the stain with a heavy duty laundry soap and soak in hot water. Wash as usual. Avoid having this problem by pouring diluted softener into the water and not directly on the clothes. Always add the softener solution to the last rinse.

DINGY, GREY, OR YELLOW DISCOLORATIONS
WASHABLE FABRICS:
Soak the clothes in hot water with twice the amount of detergent usually used. Soak several hours. Rewash in hot water with a chlorine bleach.

SHOE POLISH
WASHABLE FABRICS:

Treat stain by rubbing with a cloth dampened in turpentine or alcohol. After stain is removed, wash garment as usual.

NON-WASHABLE FABRICS:

Rub stain with a cloth dampened in turpentine or alcohol before taking to a professional dry cleaners.

CARPET:

Rub stain with a cloth dampened in turpentine or alcohol, being careful to use a circular motion.

NOTE: Cream shoe polish is much easier to remove than liquid and is best removed with turpentine. Use both procedures on liquid shoe polish.

RUST
WASHABLE FABRICS:

Wet the rust stains and rub in a bathroom cleanser which contains oxalic acid. Leave this paste on 30 minutes before washing out. Repeat if necessary.

GRASS
WASHABLE FABRICS:

Pre-treat by rubbing liquid detergent or a paste made from powdered detergent and water directly on the stain. Allow to stand several hours, then wash in hot water and a detergent.

NON-WASHABLE FABRICS:

Try to remove the stain with a dry cleaning fluid before taking the garment to a professional dry cleaners.

CARPET:

Rub a small amount of liquid detergent directly on the stain. Let stand several hours before scrubbing with a small brush. After treating with the detergent, remove all traces of it with a clean cloth wrung out with clear water.

SPOTS AND STAINS

BLOOD

WASHABLE FABRICS:

Prewash by soaking in cold water and a non-chlorine bleach. When spot is removed, wash garment in hot water and a detergent.

NON-WASHABLE FABRICS:

Before having the garment professionally cleaned, sponge with a solution of 1 ounce of household ammonia mixed in 10 ounces of water.

MILDEW

WASHABLE FABRICS:

Use either one of the following methods to remove mildew:

1. Soak mildewed garment in hot water with a chlorine bleach for 30 minutes. Wash in hot water and a detergent. If necessary, repeat this procedure.

   CAUTION: This procedure could lighten colored garments.

2. Saturate the mildewed area with lemon juice. Rub salt over the spot and place garment in the sun for several hours.

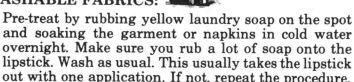

LIPSTICK

WASHABLE FABRICS:

Pre-treat by rubbing yellow laundry soap on the spot and soaking the garment or napkins in cold water overnight. Make sure you rub a lot of soap onto the lipstick. Wash as usual. This usually takes the lipstick out with one application. If not, repeat the procedure.

NON-WASHABLE FABRICS:

Before taking to a professional dry cleaners, sponge the spot with mineral spirits.

CARPET AND UPHOLSTERY:

Rub the spot with glycerine first, then with undiluted lighter fluid.

NAIL POLISH

WASHABLE FABRICS:

Scrub stain with fingernail polish remover. When the stain is removed, wash garment as usual.

NON-WASHABLE FABRICS:

Treat the stain with a cloth dampened with fingernail polish remover before sending to a professional dry cleaners.

CARPET AND UPHOLSTERY:

Treat the stain with a cloth dampened with fingernail polish remover. Rub gently with a circular motion.

CAUTION: Never use fingernail polish remover on acetate fabrics.

CORRECTION FLUID

FRESH SPILL AT THE OFFICE:

Blot immediately with a tissue. Avoid rubbing the fluid into the clothing fibers. Allow the spot to dry thoroughly, then brush with a clothes brush.

WASHABLE FABRICS:

Pre-treat the spot by rubbing with a spot and stain remover or a liquid detergent until the correction fluid is removed. Wash as usual with warm water. Check the spot after washing and before drying. If the spot remains, repeat the pre-treatment and washing. Dry in dryer only if the spot is removed since the heat could set the stain.

NON-WASHABLE FABRICS:

Rub the spot with isopropyl alcohol (without the wintergreen additive). This usually brings good results in removing the stain. First, make a patch test on an inside hem or seam to make sure there is no fabric damage or color fading. When the alcohol evaporates, it may leave a ring until the garment is dry-cleaned.

SPOTS AND STAINS

CLAY (RED)
WASHABLE FABRICS:
Wash the garment first in cold water and a detergent and then in hot water and a detergent. If the stain remains, soak garment in a gallon of hot water and 1 tablespoon of oxalic crystals. When the spot is removed, wash as usual.

CAUTION: When using oxalic acid wear rubber gloves and use in a plastic pan or pail. Never use around children since oxalic acid is poison.

NON-WASHABLE FABRICS:
Sponge spot with cold water and then send the garment to a professional cleaners.

CARPET:
Remove as much of the clay as possible with the vacuum cleaner. Then, brush the nap up and scrub vigorously with a terry cloth towel dampened with cold water and a detergent. Rinse well with clear water; rub dry. When completely dry, vacuum again. Repeat the procedure if necessary.

CANDLE WAX
WASHABLE FABRICS:
Scrape off cold wax with a knife, then press the spot between paper towels. Sponge with a dry-cleaning fluid before washing in hot water and a detergent. It may take several washings before spot is removed.

NON-WASHABLE FABRICS:
Scrape off cold wax with a knife, then press the spot between paper towels. Sponge with a dry-cleaning fluid to remove as much as possible before sending to a professional cleaners.

CARPET AND UPHOLSTERY:
Scrape off as much cold wax as possible with a knife. Sponge using a circular motion with a dry-cleaning fluid. It may take several applications before the spot is removed. Be sure to let the area dry completely between applications.

SPOTS AND STAINS

MAKE-UP

WASHABLE FABRICS:
1. Pre-treat stains from oilbased make-up by rubbing with yellow laundry soap or a liquid enzyme product. Allow to soak several hours in cold water. Wash in hot water with a detergent.
2. Pre-treat stains from waterbased make-up by soaking a short time in cold water and a mild detergent. When stain is removed, wash as usual.

NON-WASHABLE FABRICS:
Before taking to a professional dry cleaners, sponge stains from oilbased make-up with mineral spirits and stains from waterbased make-up with cold water.

PERSPIRATION

WASHABLE FABRICS:
Pre-treat by soaking in cold water with a detergent. When the stain is removed, wash garment in hot water and a detergent.

NON-WASHABLE FABRICS:
Before taking to a professional dry cleaners, sponge with cold water and a mild detergent.

CAUTION: Never try to remove perspiration stains from silk. Always take stained silk garments immediately to a professional dry cleaners.

PET STAINS AND ODORS
Pet stains and odors can be removed from carpets and upholstered furniture by following this procedure:
1. Blot stain quickly with paper towels.
2. Scrub spot vigorously with a terry cloth towel dipped in white vinegar. Be sure to squeeze excess vinegar out of towel before rubbing.
3. Rub with a circular motion.
4. When dry, fluff nap with a soft brush.

SPOTS AND STAINS ══════

MILDEW IN BATHROOMS
1. Prevent mildew by keeping things dry and clean.
2. Mildew can often be removed in bathrooms by heating damp bathrooms and allowing them to dry out thoroughly.
3. Remove musty odors caused by mildew by scrubbing the mildewed area with a solution of chlorine bleach and water (½ to 1 cup of bleach to 1 gallon of water). Rinse and wipe as dry as possible. Ventilate the area until thoroughly dry.
4. Inhibit mildew by spraying areas with a fungicide. Sprays without a fungicide may mask odors but not be effective in removing the cause of the mildew.

MILDEW ON CLOTH SHOWER CURTAINS
1. Soak mildewed shower curtain in hot water with a chlorine bleach for 30 minutes. Wash in hot water and detergent. If necessary, repeat this procedure.

   CAUTION: This procedure could lighten colored curtains.
2. Saturate the mildewed area with lemon juice. Rub salt over the spot and place curtain in the sun for several hours.

Wardrobe, Accessories, and Jewelry

WARDROBE, ACCESSORIES, AND JEWELRY

BOOTS
CLOTHES STORAGE
HANDBAGS
HEMMING
JEWELRY
LEATHER
SHOES
STOCKINGS
ZIPPERS

WARDROBE, ACCESSORIES, AND JEWELRY

JEWELRY
GENERAL HINTS:
1. Have a jeweler check your rings 3 or 4 times a year for loose stones or worn prongs.
2. Don't do housework in your rings or other fine jewelry.
3. If your rings or necklaces sometimes cause your skin to become discolored, it could be a result of hand cream, body lotion, or even the food you are eating. These things can cause precious metals to react on your skin.
4. Skin discolorations caused by a particular ring can be eliminated by coating the ring with clear fingernail polish. The polish will not damage gold or silver.

JEWELRY CONTAINERS:
Soft plastic ice cube trays make excellent containers for earrings and other small pieces of jewelry.

SAFEGUARDING JEWELRY:
1. Hide your jewelry in the freezer. Place it in an empty frozen orange juice can, replace the lid, and return the can to the freezer. Be sure to have 2 or 3 other cans of juice on the same shelf as further camouflage.
2. Hide your jewelry in the refrigerator in a refrigerator dish.

TAKING CARE OF GOLD CHAINS:
1. Don't wear your gold chains while swimming because the chlorine in water makes gold brittle.
2. Don't wear your gold chains while bathing because the washcloth could pull them out of shape or cause them to break.
3. Don't wear your gold chains while sleeping because the chains get kinks in them and could break.
4. Do keep gold chains fastened when not wearing to prevent the chains from becoming knotted.

CLEANING GOLD JEWELRY:
Gold jewelry can be cleaned in:
1 cup of water mixed with either 1 capful of ammonia or 1 capful of liquid laundry detergent or just mild detergent and water. After soaking for about 30 minutes, rinse well and dry with a lint-free cloth.

WARDROBE, ACCESSORIES, AND JEWELRY

CLEANING OPALS:

Since opals are brittle, clean them with a very soft brush and warm water. Soap or detergent is not necessary.

CLEANING PEARLS:

Clean pearls by rubbing gently with a soft, clean cloth. Never use any kind of cleaning solution on pearls. When not being worn, store your pearls in a velvet or satin-lined box.

CLEANING DIAMONDS, JADE, TOPAZ, GARNETS, AQUAMARINES, EMERALDS:

1. Wash these gems by soaking in a solution of 1 cup of water mixed with either 1 capful of ammonia or 1 capful of liquid laundry detergent for 30 minutes. Never use undiluted cleaning solutions on your jewelry.
2. After soaking, scrub gently with a soft toothbrush.
3. Rinse with clear water.
4. Dry with tissue paper or a linen cloth.

SHOES AND STOCKINGS

CLEANING BOOTS, SHOES, AND HANDBAGS MADE OF SYNTHETIC MATERIALS:

Clean boots, shoes, and handbags made of synthetic materials with a sudsy sponge. Rinse and dry thoroughly.

POLISHING SHOES:

Polish shoes by rubbing with a wedge of lemon and then buffing with a soft cloth.

NEW SHOES:

Rub the soles of new shoes with sandpaper to make them less slippery. This helps keep toddlers from falling quite as much.

WET BABY SHOES OR TENNIS SHOES:

Dry wet baby shoes and tennis shoes in a slow oven.

WHITE SHOE CLEANER:

Toothpaste makes an excellent cleaner for white shoes. Rub on and then buff.

WARDROBE, ACCESSORIES, AND JEWELRY

STOCKINGS WILL LAST LONGER:

1. When they are washed before they are ever worn.
2. If washed by hand in cold water with a mild dishwashing detergent.
3. Placed in a mesh bag and washed on the gentle cycle if machine washing is done.
4. If line-dried rather than machine dried, you can dry the stockings while still in the mesh bag. Simply hang the bag on the line.
5. If you use gloves to put on your stockings in order to avoid picks from rough hands.

STOCKING BAG:

The mesh bags used for citrus fruits or onions are excellent stocking bags.

HURRY-UP DRYING FOR STOCKINGS:

To dry stockings in a hurry, place the freshly-washed stockings on a large bath towel, roll the stockings in the towel, wring, unroll, and hang stockings on a towel rack. They dry quickly this way.

EXTRA LONG LIFE FOR STOCKINGS:

For extra long life, wrap freshly-washed stockings in foil or plastic wrap and freeze for 24 hours. After removing, let them thaw and dry in the wrap. This really extends the life of your hosiery.

STOPPING RUNS IN STOCKINGS:

Stop a run from continuing by painting the prick immediately with fingernail polish.

SAVING MONEY ON PANTYHOSE:

Always buy 2 pair of the same color pantyhose at once. When runs appear in both pair, cut off the legs with the runs and wear the two panties with their each remaining leg. Now, you have a new pair at no extra cost.

SANDALFOOT STOCKINGS:

If you cannot find the color sandalfoot stocking you need, buy a toe-in stocking in a size larger and tuck the stocking toe under your toes.

WARDROBE, ACCESSORIES, AND JEWELRY

STORING
STORING OUT-OF-SEASON CLOTHES:
1. Store clothes absolutely clean and dry. Soil weakens fibers and attracts moths.
2. Place tissue paper between garments to reduce wrinkling, add moth crystals to woolens, and place in garment bags or storage boxes with lids. Seal openings with tape.
3. Label boxes for easy access.

STORING BOOTS, SHOES, AND HANDBAGS:
Stuff boots, shoes, and handbags with paper for out-of-season storage. This will help them retain their shape. Store them in boxes to keep them dust free.

LEATHER STORAGE AND CARE:
1. Store leather goods in a cool, dry place that has good air circulation.
2. Do not store leather garments in a plastic bag.
3. Wet leather should be allowed to dry naturally.
4. When cleaning, clean all pieces of an outfit at the same time because leather may lose color when it is cleaned.

LEATHER
POLISHING LEATHER:
Use saddlesoap to polish leather articles. After applying the saddlesoap with a soft cloth, let it remain on the leather for about 30 minutes. After that length of time, brush vigorously, then buff with a cloth for shine.

CLEANING PATENT LEATHER:
Use raw biscuit dough for shining patent leather shoes or pocketbooks.

BALKY ZIPPERS:
Rub balky zippers with paraffin or candle wax to make them work more easily.

EMERGENCY HEMMING:
If the hem comes out of your pants or skirt while you are at work, "hem" them up with cellophane tape or masking tape.

INDEX

127

132

NOTES

NOTES

NOTES

NOTES